THE FAITH OF REASON

Woodbridge Prize Essay, 1947

The FAITH *of* REASON

THE IDEA OF PROGRESS IN THE FRENCH ENLIGHTENMENT

by CHARLES FRANKEL

1969
OCTAGON BOOKS
New York

Reprinted 1969
by special arrangement with Charles Frankel

OCTAGON BOOKS
A Division of Farrar, Straus & Giroux, Inc.
19 Union Square West
New York, N. Y. 10003

AM

Library of Congress Catalog Card Number: 71-86277

Printed in U.S.A. by
TAYLOR PUBLISHING COMPANY
DALLAS, TEXAS

To
HELEN

Preface

It is pleasant but difficult to record the obligations I have incurred in writing this book. I have been fortunate in having teachers who are friends, and who have communicated not only formal doctrines but something of the spirit of philosophic tolerance and integrity. What I owe to them is hard to assess because I cannot easily separate what they have given me by way of personal sympathy and support and what they have given me by way of intellectual training. Professors Irwin Edman, Horace Friess, James Gutmann, Ernest Nagel, Herbert Schneider, and John Herman Randall have all read the manuscript and helped to correct and improve it. In addition, each has aided and encouraged me in innumerable other ways. My greatest debt in the writing of this essay is to Professor Randall, who has given me the benefit at every stage of his almost frightening grasp of the history of philosophy. Professors Norman Torrey and Marjorie Nicolson have also read the manuscript and made many valuable suggestions. My wife has not only read the book as it was being written, but has lived through the writing with me. It would be difficult to say more. My debt to these men and women is so great that I feel all the more strongly my personal responsibility for what the following pages contain.

I wish to thank the following publishers for permission to quote from materials under their copyright: E. P. Dutton and Co., Rousseau's *The Social Contract and other Essays,* translated by G. D. H. Cole; Harcourt Brace and Co., *Reason and Nature,* by Morris R. Cohen; International Publishers, *Diderot: Interpreter of Nature,* translated by J. Stewart and J. Kemp; The Macmillan Company, Descartes' *Philosophical Works,* translated by E. S. Haldane and G. R. T. Ross, and *Diderot and the Encyclopedists,* by John Morley.

This book was substantially finished in the Spring of 1942. The war and the concluding of arrangements for its publication have delayed its appearance until now. If I were to do the work over again, I should undoubtedly do it differently, and I hope I would do it better. I do not feel, however, that the events of the intervening years have diminished whatever interest or importance its general theme may have had. The men with whom this book deals were among the first to attempt to mark out the ways in which western culture might successfully assimilate and control the scientific enterprise. Their attempt is an earlier episode in the history of a problem of which we are now only more urgently aware.

C. F.

New York
December, 1947

Contents

Introduction

THOMAS MALTHUS thought the Marquis de Condorcet's *Progress of the Human Mind* to be an impious and unchristian book. It suggested that man was perfectible through his own powers, not corrupt; that he needed no supernatural aid; that he could take his worldly interests at their worldly rate of exchange; that the meaning of his life could be found in this world, not in the next. Malthus opposed this blasphemous doctrine: there could be no worldly progress, but only a perpetual oscillation controlled by vice and misery and, at best, by moral restraint.

Yet in the history of ideas the underlying affinities between ideas may sometimes be stronger than, and indeed partly responsible for, their apparent opposition on the surface, and it is significant that Malthus' doctrine passed by easy stages into the nineteenth-century creed of progress, where it merged with ideas inherited from the French liberals of the eighteenth century. There was probably more in common between Malthus and Condorcet than either would have suspected. The eighteenth-century *philosophes* opposed universal reason to special revelation, and man's natural powers and interests to his supernatural salvation and destiny. They opposed the sanctions of mere tradition and appealed to each individual's sense of the truth, to his desocialized reason, stripped of its prejudices and distrust of itself. But the *philosophes* were often more traditional than they thought, and many of their conclusions came from unquestioned habits of mind which had a long tradition before them. The *philosophes* could read reason as itself a revelation, and find a support for man's natural interests in the fortuitous—one might say, providential—appropriateness with which human strivings fit the Order of Nature. And they could persist in a separation of the goal or meaning of life from the present character of their experience which was not unlike a more traditional otherworldliness. In the eighteenth century, as Voltaire said, men cried, "All is well," in a mournful voice. It required no great stretching of doctrine for men a century later, watching the struggle for survival Malthus had pictured, to cry cheerfully, "All is pain."

It is one of the purposes of the present work to relate the *philosophes'* ideas on progress to the larger metaphysical prepossessions which they inherited. One object of the history of ideas is to extricate from the chronology of beliefs those elements which show greater staying power, whether they be certain habits of inference, or certain unperceived metaphors or analogies, or unconscious assumptions and selective emphases, and to show how older ideas have been reformulated in the light of new events and new events assimilated to older and more comfortable forms. By noting the presence of these elements which show greater resistance to change we can provide structure and continuity to what would otherwise be merely a chronicle of the order in which changes have succeeded one another.

The beliefs that reason was absolute, that nature was harmonious, and that the end, once attained, would retroactively justify the means, were among the consequences of a particular metaphysical frame of reference which the *philosophes* inherited, and which they unconsciously shared with many of those whom they opposed. These beliefs provided one aspect of the faith of reason which was expressed through ideas of progress—namely, the conviction held by believers in reason that reason had the exclusive, or at least predominant, support of the external environment.

The faith of reason was, however, a complex and uneasy combination of beliefs, and it contained elements which were the distinctive products of new experience and which were potentially disruptive of older forms. Many of the *philosophes* struggled with their metaphysics, and some of them succeeded in moving beyond it. Although the *philosophes,* who were propagandists, had the habit of proposing either-or alternatives, it is sometimes misleading to take them at their word. It is worth remembering that their great contemporary critic Rousseau was himself a *philosophe,* and had their habit of posing hard and fast alternatives. There was more than one element embodied in the *philosophes'* ideas of progress, and their notions of reason and science were larger and less single-minded than their own polemics, and equally polemical criticism, have sometimes permitted them to seem.

The new elements which were brought into focus by the idea of progress were the products of the emergence in Europe of a new method of institutionalized inquiry. The development of ideas on progress was an incident in the appearance of modern mathematico-experimental science. Ideas of progress emerged in the attempt to understand the social implications of this event, to define the status of science with respect to other institutions, rooted in tradition or revelation or police-power, and to establish the right of scientific inquiry to invade any of these fields. Out of this struggle there emerged, in addition to the interpretation that established science as simply a new and better version of the old, absolute type of authority, another interpretation of science which gave a different meaning to the idea of progress. Science was a revolutionary institution, and the peculiar instrument of progress, because it embodied a new kind of authority which, unlike any other authority, was internally progressive and improved with use.

Underlying the ideas of the *philosophes* on progress were thus two widely divergent interpretations of science, two different notions of its nature and relationship to older dispensations. The one, combining elements drawn from Descartes with ideas drawn from empiricist sources, placed science in a larger metaphysical context, attempted to establish its validity as an instrument of progress unprovisionally by basing it on absolute grounds external to the method of science itself, and defined progress in terms of the movement toward fixed moral goals which were also established absolutely; the other, which, as we shall see, found an early seventeenth-century representative in Blaise Pascal, drew its interpretation of science not from antecedent metaphysical principles, but from the *method* of science itself, argued that the use of this method required no external, absolute justification because it was itself self-corrective, and implied, consequently, that the persisting goal of science need not be anything external to it, but simply the preservation and extension of the conditions and methods of inquiry. Although these two interpretations of science were not always clearly distinguished from each other, and, indeed, were often maintained side by side, the differences between them were great: the first defined the progressiveness of science in terms of its approach to goals established absolutely by other than the provisional methods of science, while the second defined progress in terms of the approach of social behavior to the kind of behavior exhibited by the progressive method of science itself.

This essay deals with these ideas of science, and with their consequences in ideas of progress. After an initial consideration of the social context which stimulated reflection on progress, this study will examine the primary source in the seventeenth century of the one view of progress in the philosophy of Descartes, and, for purposes of contrast, the view of Pascal, which provides a foretaste of the second view of progress. It will then proceed to analyze, in the philosophy of Condillac, the way in which the *philosophes* used essential elements in the Cartesian ideas of science and progress, while restating them in empiricist language, and will move on to the further development of these ideas in utilitarian and materialist theories of progress. The discussion will then turn to attempts to move beyond the confines of the narrower, metaphysical faith of reason, and to a consideration of the interplay, in the histories written during the period, between absolute conceptions of science and the emerging historical awareness of its social context and incidence. The discussion will conclude with the philosophy of Condorcet, in which these various movements of ideas all come to a kind of summation.

Such an essay is not concerned with the technical philosophy of science, but rather with reflections upon the relationship of science to society and morals, and, moreover, with only one comparatively brief episode in the history of such reflections. Nevertheless, even though it concentrates upon an idea which is now used by many primarily to characterize a mistaken faith of the recent past, a writer may be pardoned if he hopes that such a study is not without some larger bearing. For the idea of human improvement through the use of organized intelligence is still central to liberal philosophies. It was through the idea of progress that the *philosophes* expressed the social implications of the emergence of the institutionalized method of inquiry represented by science. The awareness of science which they promoted has become a kind of magnetic pole from which the contemporary liberal imagination takes direction.

As an examination of these men may reveal, it is not science, however, but the interpretation of science which limits or extends the scope and character of what that imagination will entertain. It is for this reason that the discrimination of the various conceptions of science within the theories of progress held by the *philosophes* may have some relevance to the present situation of liberal beliefs. Rational control of human affairs that will not reduce moral quality to quantity, programs of social reform that will not envisage human problems as problems simply for mechanical manipulation—these are among the encircling dilemmas of the contemporary liberal. They were also the problems of the eighteenth-century men who consolidated the liberal faith.

The Philosophic Century

*Our century has called itself the
philosophic century* par excellence.
(D'Alembert)

THE IMPACT OF THE NEW SCIENCE

"I DO not know whether I have too favorable an opinion of my century, but it seems to me that there is a certain fermentation of universal reason which is tending to develop, and which perhaps will be allowed to dissipate itself, the progress of which could be assured, directed and hastened by skillful cultivation."[1] In the year 1751, Charles Duclos' opinion of his century merely reinforced what most enlightened men already felt. In passing judgment on his age Duclos was himself illustrating its modernity, and calling attention to a social process of steadily emerging significance—a fermentation of universal reason, bubbling out from a common center, flowing in a definite direction, and dissolving old faiths. It was the year in which the *Encyclopædia* appeared as a joint enterprise of "philosophic spirits," and as the climax of five years of remarkable vitality, marked by the publication of Voltaire's *Essai sur les mœurs,* Condillac's *Essai sur les origines des connaissances humaines,* and other books using similar critical tools in a common purpose, and speaking with a peculiar excitement of what had been accomplished and what might yet be done. The scalpel of a new intellectual method was being sharpened in order to lay bare "the anatomy of the soul" and of society.

1. Duclos, *Œuvres,* I, 55.

It seemed to men that Isaac Newton had brought the edifice of science almost to the point of completion. Economical in its architecture and comprehensive in what it enclosed, it gave men reason to stop and think about the slapped-together Shantytowns that enclosed their political and social lives. They were already restive under the cost of religious wars fought for the right to be called Christian or for the power to monopolize the title, and they were already bemused in their expanding world by the discovery of societies that were not Christian or European at all. They were already straining at having to maintain an expensive dynasty and the doddering privileged class which that dynasty had shorn of real function—"the whipped cream of Europe," Voltaire called it. And now, if Newton had unseated Aristotle, what were men to think of other authorities they had inherited? If so much could be done to understand the physical world, what might be done to solve perplexing human problems? Science might become a social and political power, a solvent of hardened customs and traditions and a means of organizing happier human arrangements.

Two great traditions, humanism and science, came together in the eighteenth century. The first had acquired a weapon, the second a conscience: together they constituted a revolutionary program. The outlines of this program had been suggested in 1690, only three years after the appearance of Newton's *Principia Mathematica,* by John Locke, whose *Essay Concerning Human Understanding* had shown the bearing of the new science upon human concerns. Reminding his readers that "morality is the proper study and business of mankind in general," Locke had expressed the hope that "from self-evident propositions, by necessary consequences, as incontestible as those in mathematics, the measures of right and wrong might be made out." [2]

Perhaps history as a tale of crime and folly might come to its close in this age of enlightenment. For if, as Matthew Arnold said, modernity is "the tendency to observe facts with a critical spirit," this was an age that made modernity a profession. Jean D'Alembert, editor of the *Encyclopædia,* wrote, "Philosophy is nothing else than the application of reason to the different objects on which it can be exercised," and his was the most philosophic of centuries:

2. Locke, *Essay,* II, 351, 208.

Every century that does any thinking at all—whether it be good or bad—provided that it believes that it thinks, and that it thinks differently from the century that preceded it, decorates itself with the title, philosophic. . . . Our century has therefore called itself the *philosophic century* par excellence. . . . From the principles of the profane sciences to the foundations of revelation, from metaphysics to questions of taste, from music to morals, from the scholastic disputes of theologians to commercial affairs, from the rights of princes to those of peoples, from the natural law to the arbitrary law of nations, in a word, from the questions that affect us most to those that interest us least, everything has been discussed, analyzed, disputed.[3]

THE NEW ROLE OF THE INTELLECTUAL

What was significant was that restlessness, fermentation, and modernity were no longer merely the characteristics of self-consciously isolated individuals like Erasmus. They were the qualities of a group, the temper of a company of men engaging in a coöperative endeavor like the *Encyclopædia.* The Age of Enlightenment is the age in which men tried systematically to convert enlightenment from something that had been largely a personal affair, lackadaisical, sporadic, and accidental, into a cultural and political process that could be organized and controlled. A learned class was emerging in a new role and relationship to the rest of society.

The men who took part in this event regarded it as the distinctive hall-mark of their age, a shift in social relationships which was of seminal importance, and it was in interpreting the meaning of this event that ideas of progress emerged during the period. Through the idea of progress the sources, the tasks, and the prospects of the intellectual class were explored. The *philosophes* tried to provide a philosophy for intellectuals in the eighteenth century in the way that Marx tried to provide one for the proletariat a century later.

The attitude of these intellectuals of the eighteenth century towards their vocation and its place contained three principal elements. The intellectual was morally dedicated to humanity; he regarded science as a powerful social weapon of which he was the distinctive trustee; and he thought that intellectuals formed a distinct and unified class

3. D'Alembert, *Œuvres,* II, 9–11.

with a common social program. Professional intellectuals had, so to speak, joined the human race. In the words of Diderot, "Our philosopher . . . is full of humanity. Civil society is, so to say, a divinity for him on earth; he honours it by his probity, by an exact attention to his duties, and by a sincere desire not to be a useless or an embarrassing member of it." [4] The scientific revolution was important to the *philosophes* as a human creation. It opened new vistas in the physical world; but it also made men reflect on how much human beings could achieve. Banish man from the universe, as Diderot wrote in his article, *"Encyclopédie,"* and the sublime spectacle of nature becomes melancholy and silent. It is the fact that man is part of nature that makes all the rest of nature interesting. Why not, then, make man the point from which we set out to study nature and the point to which we trace everything back? Why not make the laws of the growth and progress of human intelligence the principles by which all our sciences are unified? As the diverse enterprises of the Middle Ages came together in the drama of salvation and were crowned by "the journey of the mind to God," so the intellectual wanderings of the Enlightenment came together in "the progress of the human mind."

The new attitude, however, is not reducible to the exhortation that the intellectual ought to leave his cloister once in a while and be a citizen. Rather, it lies in a new recognition that science and criticism have a social function even if the individual thinker is unaware of it. The *philosophes* were conscious that they were living through an intellectual revolution—a revolution among intellectuals—and they did not feel that the result of this revolution was simply that the man of books had come to be reminded that he had other obligations and that he also ought to be a man of action. Rather, the revolution lay in the discovery that when a man is properly intellectual he is in that way performing a social function and engaging in a species of social action. The *philosophes* thought that science might become the acknowledged legislator (as well as the technologist) of the human race, and they believed that they were exercising a political function when they wrote as men of letters for the *Encyclopædia*. The basis of their program was simply the belief that if a culture were submitted to scientific examination it might become less illiberal and superstitious. Intellec-

4. Quoted by Martin, *French Liberal Thought*, p. 92.

tuals should address themselves to this task, and, in doing so, should keep themselves in character as intellectuals. D'Alembert described the manner and program of action proper to the intellectual:

Happy are men of letters if they recognize at last that the surest way of making themselves respectable is to live united and almost shut up among themselves; that by this union they will come, without any trouble, to give the law to the rest of the nation in all affairs of taste and philosophy. . . . As if the art of instructing and enlightening men were not, after the too rare art of good government, the noblest portion and gift in human reach.[5]

This was the distinctive task of the intellectual class, a task which no other class could perform, and which the intellectual class could not perform if it was subservient to patronage or spread its energies by failing in class-consciousness. Men of letters might now instruct and not merely ornament a culture. It is true that we can now find much that seems to be merely special pleading in the work of the *philosophes.* Nevertheless, they were in their own minds concerned predominantly with showing their contemporaries the inherent virtue of free inquiry; and to be self-consciously Socratic as a class represented a significant development in the social function of the man of letters. It was the "philosophic spirit" (and not any special interest) which the *philosophes* thought they represented, and which the *Encyclopædia* predicted would "spread . . . its influence through the whole system of the state, through all the works of the hand or of the mind." [6] The Enlightenment was a movement among intellectuals to assert themselves as a social force and to attempt to introduce, or at least to talk about, a new technique of social change.

In this historic mission the intellectual classes seemed now to be unified. Professional intellectuals in France in the eighteenth century had come to take themselves seriously enough to regard themselves as a coöperative group in which individual differences on speculative issues were relatively unimportant when compared to the major agreements concerning common tools and objectives. Condorcet, who provided the best contemporary account of the social policies of the man of letters, observed that intellectuals presented a common front to the rest of society: "The philosophers of different nations, embracing in

5. Translated by Morley, *Diderot,* I, 129.
6. See the article, "L'esprit philosophique," in the *Encyclopédie.*

their meditations the entire interests of man, without distinction of country, of color, or of sect, formed . . . a firm and united phalanx against every description of error, every species of tyranny." [7] The idea of progress expressed the implications of the emergence of this class with its special weapon, science, and provided a setting in history and in the laws of nature in terms of which this event might be understood and properly appreciated.

THE DISTINCTIVE QUALITY OF THE FRENCH ENLIGHTENMENT

It was in France that enlightenment had its most lively career, and it was from France, which was the social center of the Enlightenment, that such tenets of enlightenment as the belief in progress were most widely disseminated. The Enlightenment was a movement that transcended national boundaries; it fostered and was in turn sustained by a European culture. But there were, nevertheless, national variations. Although in Scotland philosophy gradually developed a skeptical and radical tendency in metaphysics, the Enlightenment in Britain as a whole was relatively conservative. The Glorious Revolution had created an attitude of having arrived, a confident sense that the Constitution and the Whigs were safe, which made the representatives of English Enlightenment glorifiers of an achievement, and not prophets of a revolution. Where there was a radical strain it was confined largely to religious issues and did not extend to criticism of political affairs. Utilitarianism, for example, which became such a potent weapon for social reform in nineteenth-century England, began in England as an appendage to theology and became radical only after it had passed through the hands of the French.

The Enlightenment in Germany also varied from that in France, being largely formal and academic. The philosophy of Leibniz grew out of a predominant concern with the mathematical side of the new sciences, and, in the shape given to it by Christian Wolff's rationalistic metaphysics, it exercised a controlling influence over the German Enlightenment. The German Enlightenment was stirred out of an in-

---

7. Condorcet, *The Progress of the Human Mind*, p. 256.

cipient scholasticism by poet-philosophers like Lessing and Goethe, by the skepticism of Hume, and by the infiltration of French ideas that helped to push the movement closer to practical affairs.

In contrast with these tendencies, the French Enlightenment was both a revolutionary portent and a political weapon. The basic intellectual materials of the Enlightenment came from England, but its moral animation came from France. Voltaire might go to England as a poet and leave as a philosopher; but a British or German philosopher would leave France as a propagandist. Espousing the very same liberties, an eighteenth-century Englishman was on the side of the *status quo* and a Frenchman was subversive of an *ancien régime*. "One must disguise at Paris what I could not say too strongly at London," wrote Voltaire.[8] The *philosophes* were cosmopolitan in an era of competing national states; they talked of natural rights while political institutions were grounded in divine right and buttressed by ecclesiastical authority; they argued that the real source of political authority was the "general will" when the monarchs of Europe were continuing to regard their realms as family possessions. In the same fashionable *salons* that helped Helvétius write his books there was also present an affected skepticism like that of the Abbé Coignard, who objected to the Declaration of the Rights of Man "because of the excessive and unfair separation it established between man and the gorilla."

The radical separation of the *philosophes* from the situation they were trying to correct was undoubtedly responsible in part for the dualism between "reason" and "experience" which, as we shall see, played so large a role in their theories of progress. There were practical and literary reasons—the censorship, the prestige of science—to impel the *philosophes* to adopt a universal manner of utterance; and there was much in the rigidity of the *ancien régime* to impel them to combat the authority of Revelation with the revelation of other authorities which, if new, were no less unbending. Under these circumstances, the characteristic metaphysical dualism of the man who had observed that "good sense is, of all things among men, the most equally distributed," was, especially when its language was changed, extremely well fitted to the purposes of criticism, and it is to René Descartes' metaphysics that we must now turn.

8. Quoted by Morley, *Voltaire*, p. 64.

The New Method of Philosophy

The new method of philosophy was first introduced into the world by the famous Descartes. . . . 'Twas then indeed, it might justly be said, that . . . a God had come down to clear this chaos, dissipate the darkness, and create light. (Terrasson)

THE *PHILOSOPHES* AND DESCARTES

THE special position which the *philosophes* gave to Descartes, despite the frequency and vigor with which they attacked his speculative metaphysics, provides a clue to the character of his influence upon them. In general, Descartes' influence on the French Enlightenment did not produce philosophies that announced themselves as Cartesian.[1] It was not to Descartes, but to Francis Bacon, Newton, and Locke that the *philosophes* turned when they looked for exemplars of proper intellectual method. At the same time that the great works in social criticism written during the fifth decade of the century were attacks upon the superstitions of the *ancien régime,* they were also, for the most part, revolts against the Cartesian reinforcement of supernaturalism—the separation of the mind from physical nature. The *philosophes* stressed the fact that they had broken with Cartesianism as a system:

1. D'Alembert wrote in 1750: "The present situation of this great man Descartes is such that, after having had innumerable partisans, he is now . . . reduced to a few apologists." (*Œuvres,* I, 284.) See Fontenelle's *Histoire de l'Académie des Sciences* (1731) for a contemporary account of the impact of Newton on Cartesianism.

Descartes, as Voltaire and others wrote, had discovered the mistakes of antiquity, but he had substituted his own in their place. In following Locke, who had "reduced metaphysics to what it ought to be in fact, the experimental physics of the soul," the *philosophes* had ceremoniously rejected Descartes' "metaphysical romance." [2]

But in the last analysis Descartes seems to have been criticized because, after all, he had not been Cartesian enough. In 1687, Bishop Bossuet had written to a friend that Cartesianism was more than just another heresy, that it was a manifestation of a general spirit of unbelief. If this was Cartesianism, then Descartes, the *philosophes* felt, had not himself been a thoroughgoing Cartesian. For the *philosophes* remembered him as the revolutionary who had made doubting a systematic affair, and as the seer who had revealed the possibility of making mathematics a universal method for all the sciences; consequently, in having separated the mind from the world of measurable things, Descartes could be accused of having failed to carry through the very program he had initiated. In arguing that there was a substance—*res cogitans,* the mind—to which mathematical method was wholly inappropriate, Descartes had given a metaphysical sanction to the existing social barriers against the extension of free, scientific inquiry into religious, political, and moral domains. That authorities claiming a basis in a super-rational revelation exercised a virtual monopoly of power over social arrangements was something which the *philosophes* recognized to be a fact. But Cartesian metaphysics seemed an attempt to celebrate this recognized matter of fact as an illustration of a necessary and inescapable law. At the very least, Cartesianism had tended to become an elaborate new scholasticism which was a distraction from the important practical business of philosophy; and in certain cases—witness Bishop Bossuet's defense of divine-right absolutism— it had also been used to support the claims of supernatural theology to authority over morals and politics.

So Voltaire could prefer Locke because the Englishman was more Cartesian, more consistently mathematical-minded, than Descartes

2. D'Alembert, *Œuvres,* I, 276. The *philosophes* of course continued to regard Descartes' analytic geometry as "the key to the most important discoveries." See D'Alembert's *Preliminary Discourse* to the *Encyclopédie.*

himself. Descartes had lost himself in speculation, and had surrendered his program of applying scientific methods to the study of man; but Locke had pushed forward to uncover "the anatomy of the soul" by placing it within the world of physical bodies in motion. Proceeding from "well-established facts" and rejecting speculative hypotheses, Locke had nevertheless managed to retain the geometrical manner of analysis, and had shown that, without the smallest assistance from geometry, a man might still possess a truly geometrical intellect.[3]

But if Descartes had not been consistent he had nevertheless set the pattern; and the *philosophes* recognized that Locke and the other luminaries of the Enlightenment were his heirs. When the *philosophes* tried to see themselves in the setting of history, when they tried to connect their program with its sources, they recognized Descartes as a pivotal figure in the progress of the human mind. Descartes had given the first considerable impetus to the onslaught against the unquestioning acceptance of inherited beliefs. His systematic doubt had dramatized the career of the individual's liberated mind confronting a world that it had never made. "Until he appeared the study of nature was benumbed, spiritless, and inert. . . . Descartes at least dared to show . . . how to overthrow scholasticism, opinion, authority, in a word, prejudice and barbarism; and through that revolt . . . Philosophy was rendered a service by him." [4]

Even so relatively conservative a man as Turgot, who stressed the importance to the progress of mankind of Christianity in particular, and of historic continuity in general, recognized the contribution Descartes had made simply as a revolutionary, as a man who had demonstrated the importance and possibility of destroying inherited notions that interfered with the progress of investigation.[5] For the *philosophes* agreed that a new approach to the past was necessary, and the consolidation of this approach they took to be the distinctive achievement of their most philosophic of centuries. In Descartes' con-

---

3. See Voltaire, *Works,* XIII, 99.   4. Article, "Descartes," *Encyclopédie.*
5. "What mortal dared to reject the insights of all past ages, and even the ideas he believed most certain? It is as if he wanted to extinguish the torch of the sciences so that he could relight it all by himself with the pure fire of reason. . . . Great Descartes, if it was not always given to you to find the truth, you did at least destroy tyranny and error." (Turgot, *Œuvres,* II, 89.)

viction that the mind must be purged of the corrupting influence of the past they found a precursor of their own self-conscious "modernity."

Furthermore, the specific purge which the *philosophes* used—"the analytic method"—bore a recognized affinity with the method of Descartes. The methodical breaking down of complex ideas into simple, presumably irreducible, sense-impressions displayed, as the Abbé de Condillac observed, and as we shall see in greater detail in Chapter III, the persistence of the mathematical method of Descartes. Even though the *philosophes* looked upon themselves as "empiricists" rather than "rationalists," and thought that the ultimate elements of ideas were sense-impressions rather than self-evident ideas, they shared the basic Cartesian assurance that the human understanding might be solidly reconstructed exclusively out of the simple elements revealed by analysis.

The *philosophes* regarded Descartes, furthermore, as the first great exponent not merely of analysis but of the mechanistic ideal that all nature might be explained in the terms of a universal science of mechanics.

It was Descartes who . . . made a revolution. The system of occasional causes, the idea of reducing everything to matter and motion, are the main principles of this vigorous philosopher, and imply an analysis of ideas of which the Ancients afforded no example. . . . Locke succeeded in pushing this analysis very much farther. Berkeley and Condillac followed him. They are all children of Descartes.[6]

If the *philosophes* did not agree with each of Descartes' arguments in support of this method of analysis they accepted his metaphysical conclusion concerning the absolute ontological status of that method. The idea of reducing everything to matter and motion was a way of eliminating as "irrational" or "unnatural" what could not be so reduced. The *philosophes* sought, as did Descartes, to establish the validity of ideas by showing them to be entirely composed of irreducible simples (albeit clear and distinct "sensations" rather than clear and distinct ideas) always and everywhere available to men, and to liberate the human mind by purging it of the contingent, the historical, the "un-

6. D'Alembert, *Œuvres*, I, 278. See Picavet, *Les idéologues*, pp. 4 ff.

clear" notions that were the accidents of a particular education in a particular time and place.

Even though the *philosophes* thought they had shifted from "rationalism" to "empiricism," their main metaphysical assumption thus remained Cartesian in an important respect. The "analytic method" of the *philosophes* was not simply a method for investigating the origins of beliefs and ideas. The results it obtained were evaluated in the light of a prepossession about what was ultimate and constant in the universe: the products of analysis—simple sensations—were the invariable ingredients of all experience. Consequently, what was left over and unaccounted for after analysis into simples was temporary, relative, and invalid. It was "mere" custom, accidental and unreasonable. In terms of this prepossession the analytic method functioned not primarily as a way of investigating the historic development of ideas but rather as a disinfectant intended to rid men of ill-founded or irrational beliefs. Further, the analytic method was the method of *esprits simplistes*. What could not be taken account of by analysis need not be taken account of. The *philosophes* preferred simplicity and took it to be an essential touchstone of validity. The ability to attain solutions that were simple was one of the marks of a good intellectual method and one of the tests of the success of any course of investigation. Not merely must the ultimate elements of ideas be simple, but taken together they ought not to be complicated. Perhaps man cannot know everything. But he may be confident that the problems he can solve require no extraordinary ability, nothing much more than the good sense (which is "of all things in the world most equally distributed") to see through complications. As Professor Lovejoy has observed,[7] the mental habit of the *esprit simpliste* was one of the more pervasive controlling presumptions of the Enlightenment. It was important precisely because it was so easily and so widely taken for granted. If the *philosophes* joined Locke in the belief that man's knowledge was limited, they also shared his conviction that man could know enough for the purposes of enlightened behavior, and they agreed with Descartes that what man did know could be easily grasped and simply demonstrated. As Professor Gilson has pointed out, mathematics had been recognized as the most certain science before Descartes, but only

7. Lovejoy, *The Great Chain of Being*, pp. 7–10.

Descartes had insisted upon taking it as the exclusive model for all science and denying value to whatever could not attain equal simplicity and certainty. His belief in the universality of the mathematical method was what distinguished Descartes from his predecessors and made him a revolutionary. From the point of view of medieval philosophy he was *"indisciplinatus,"* one who "makes it a point to seek in no matter what discipline a degree of certainty that it does not allow." [8] It was with this ideal of science, with its "radical elimination of the probable," that Descartes exerted his fundamental influence on the *philosophes,* and we must consequently turn to consider it in greater detail and to examine its bearings on ideas of progress.

DESCARTES' IDEAL OF SCIENCE AND STANDARD OF PROGRESS

Descartes was primarily a mathematician and physicist [9] who wanted to explain all events in nature in terms of universal laws mathematically formulated. The event which he recognized as the decisive turning point of his career was the revelation that came to him in November, 1619, that a universal mathematics was possible. From that time on, he was a consistent mathematical physicist who, like Galileo, eliminated scholastic concepts from his procedures and employed the quantitative concept of extension.

Nevertheless, Descartes was never satisfied to be merely a physicist. After 1619 he continued to develop a mathematical physics, but he felt that he was proceeding only tentatively and provisionally until, nine years later, he had worked out a metaphysical philosophy which provided an external foundation for his mathematical method. To proceed tentatively and provisionally seemed not enough to Descartes. He frequently criticized Galileo for his lack of a metaphysical system, and he blamed Galileo's errors in physics on his failure to inquire into

8. Gilson, *La pensée mediévale dans la système cartésien,* pp. 234–35.
9. Descartes' method as a working physicist was mathematico-experimental, like Galileo's. See Hyman Stock, *The Method of Descartes in the Natural Sciences,* especially pp. 66 ff.

"the first causes of nature." [10] And despite the success Descartes enjoyed with the mathematical method in physics, it was only after Descartes had developed his metaphysics that he felt free to undertake a direct attack upon the scholastic doctrine of substantial forms.

Descartes wanted to inquire in an orderly way, to build upon solid foundations. And this seemed to him to require infallible principles logically prior to his physics, principles which would justify his setting aside all other methods and holding his own up as the only path to truth. Descartes developed his metaphysical dualism in order to vindicate the elimination of all other than the mathematical. His metaphysics made the preferences of the *esprit simpliste* categorical.

That Descartes should have felt that his method was insufficiently established until he had based it upon prior indubitable allegations such as the existence of God, that he should, in other words, have felt that his physics was incomplete without metaphysics, is a consequence of the ideal of science which he held. For while Descartes was interested in displaying a world that was all matter in motion, he retained the preoccupation of a man of the Middle Ages with setting his spirit at rest. He wanted a Universal Wisdom which would give everything its place in a necessary and finished scheme of things. Even while proposing a revolutionary new method, he held the medieval ideal of a monolithic science, arguing that philosophy must be conceived as a unit: "Philosophy as a whole is like a tree whose roots are metaphysics, whose trunk is physics, and whose branches, which issue from this trunk, are all the other sciences." [11] Descartes placed physics within an over-all system, and he judged the meaning as well as the validity of physics in the terms provided by this logically antecedent, and independently established, metaphysics. Physics was completed in philosophy.

In the preface to his *Principles of Philosophy* Descartes defined phi-

10. Descartes, *Œuvres,* II, 380. (Letter to Mersenne, October 11, 1638.) Descartes expresses agreement with Galileo's attempt to give a mathematical account of physical matters, but goes on to add, "It seems to me that Galileo falls very short in that he . . . does not stop to explain a matter entirely, . . . and, without considering the first causes of nature, he seeks only for the reasons for certain particular effects, so that he builds without a foundation."

11. Descartes, *Philosophical Works,* I, 211.

losophy as the study of wisdom; "and by that wisdom we not only understand prudence in affairs, but also a perfect knowledge of all things that man can know, both for the conduct of his life and for the conservation of his health and the invention of all the arts." This wisdom is "none other than the knowledge of the truth through its first causes." It is the supreme good of human life—an intellectual excellence distinctively fitted to the nature of man, "in whom the principal part is the mind," and at the same time a virtue of practical importance, "more necessary for the regulation of our manners and for our conduct of life than is the use of our eyes in the guidance of our steps." [12] Universal Wisdom was the goal of Descartes' new method.

Natural science was of course of much greater intrinsic interest to Descartes than it was to St. Augustine or, for that matter, to most of the *philosophes*. But Descartes' concern with the moral import of the new science was among the antecedents of the *philosophes'* concern for the effect of science upon happiness. Descartes had a pronounced moral interest which is unmistakable in his autobiographical account of his intellectual development, and he gave it the place of an ultimate standard in his philosophical system. "I have always had an excessive desire to learn to distinguish the true from the false," he wrote in the *Discourse on Method,* "in order to see clearly in my actions and to walk with confidence in this life."

Descartes' practical interest in science was not primarily an interest in what has since come to be called "applied science." His objection, for example, to mathematics as it was taught at La Flèche was not that it was an instrument of scholasticism but that it was used exclusively for specialized technical ends.[13] In his "first rule for the direction of the mind" he criticized "honorable and laudable pursuits" like "those sciences conducive to the conveniences of life." But he also criticized the sciences "which yield that pleasure which is found in the contemplation of truth." Both were misleading because both gave rise to specialized interests that prevent the realization of the proper goal of the sciences. Descartes pushed his subordination of the special sciences to a higher unity very far in theory. The first rule for the direc-

12. *Ibid.,* pp. 203–5.

13. *Ibid.,* p. 85. "I was astonished that, seeing how firm and solid was its basis, no loftier edifice had been reared thereupon."

tion of the mind requires that the unity of the sciences never be forgotten. "The sciences taken all together are identical with human wisdom," and good understanding or Universal Wisdom is the supreme goal of science to which any minor purpose must be sacrificed. "All other studies are to be esteemed not so much for their own value as because they contribute something to this." The search after such wisdom must be the ever-present driving principle in scientific progress, its final cause, so to speak. And in the last analysis this search after wisdom, this endeavor to increase the natural light of reason, which is the all-embracing purpose of science, has a moral justification. As for the *philosophes* so for Descartes, enlightenment was ultimately a practical tool directing the will "to its proper choice in all the contingencies of life." [14]

It is wisdom, so conceived, that provided Descartes' measure of progress. In the preface to his *Principles of Philosophy* Descartes considered the question of progress fairly specifically. In explaining the subject matter of the *Principles of Philosophy,* his design in writing the book, and the use to be derived from it, Descartes specified the respects in which his system was "new," and why it was better than the "old." In this essay Descartes established the level attained by philosophy as the touchstone of the value of a civilization:

Since it extends over the whole range of human knowledge, we are entitled to hold that it alone is what distinguishes us from savages and barbarians, and that the civilization and refinement of each nation is proportionate to the superiority of its philosophy. In this way a state can have no greater good than the possession of true philosophy. [15]

And such true philosophy was now made available by the mathematical method. In this view of the nature and importance of philosophy we have the forerunner of the position of the *philosophes*—their assimilation of human progress in general to the progress of human enlightenment in particular, and their interpretation of enlightenment as the possession of a unified system of infallible truths deduced from a few simple premises. For while Descartes emphasized the practice of Method itself, and the consequent promotion of good understanding, as the predominant goal of science, the Method for Descartes was

14. *Ibid.,* pp. 1–2. (Rule I, *Rules for the Direction of the Mind.*)
15. *Ibid.,* p. 204.

more than mathematics, or the four steps he proposed in the *Discourse on Method*. It was these ways of inquiry *plus* certain metaphysical allegations concerning their absolute validity.

Furthermore, the notion that moral wisdom was the culminating contribution of the new enlightenment was also foreshadowed by Descartes. The last degree of wisdom, its culminating point, was moral science, which presupposes "a complete knowledge of the other sciences." [16] The medieval notion that knowledge could be completely summed up, together with its Augustinian emphasis that the sum would be moral, was passed down to the Enlightenment by Descartes in the shape of the conviction that moral progress was to be made (and was now possible) by deducing an infallible moral science from the other branches of knowledge. The memory of Descartes is revived by Condorcet's remark that every error in politics goes back to an error in physics. To say that scientific theories may influence a moral outlook, or that the application of scientific theories affects human relationships, is one thing; to say that a specific metaphysical or physical theory logically implies an ethical program is something else again. It was Hume who finally disturbed the Enlightenment in the assurance it shared with Descartes that there was a necessary connection between "reason" and "value."

THE NEW PHILOSOPHY AND THE OLD

Descartes' criticisms of the traditional philosophy of the Schools were for the most part recapitulated in the *Discourse on Method*. He found the old philosophy to be overly subtle and endlessly argumentative, and his studies "had no other effect than the increasing discovery of his own ignorance." Notwithstanding the efforts of centuries, traditional philosophy had not made a single affirmation "which is not subject of dispute, and in consequence which is not dubious." [17] Indeed, we are reminded by Descartes' discussion in the *Rules for the Direction of the Mind* that past philosophy would have been uncertain even if it showed one long record of agreement. "Even though all these men agreed among themselves, what they teach us would not

16. *Ibid.*, p. 211.   17. *Ibid.*, pp. 83, 86.

suffice for us." [18] The philosophy of the Schools was uncertain not simply because everything in it was a matter of dispute, but because it offered not a single principle which could be employed as the basis of an indubitable proposition, and consequently had no way of settling these disputes. Consequently, the philosophy taught in the Schools was not merely unprogressive in fact; it was inherently unprogressive, that is, incapable of moving toward certainty. Traditional philosophy was arid, and irrelevant to the central philosophic business of progressive discovery of truth. "I observed in respect to Logic that the syllogisms and the greater part of the other teaching served better in explaining to others those things that one knows . . . than in learning what is new." [19]

In the preface to the *Principles* Descartes described succinctly "in what all the knowledge we now possess consists, and to what degree of wisdom we have attained," and then went on to explain in what way his own system represented a revolutionary event in the progress of philosophy. The wisdom we possess has been usually acquired in one or another of four ways: from immediately clear notions, from sense-experience, from conversation, and from books. But there has also been a fifth way, "incomparably more elevated and assured than these other four."

That road is to seek out the first causes and the true principles from which reasons may be deduced for all that which we are capable of knowing; and it is those who have made this their special work who have been called philosophers. At the same time I do not know that up to the present day there have been any in whose case this plan has succeeded.[20]

Descartes' philosophy was "new" and "progressive" because it had succeeded where everyone else had failed. It represented the successful achievement of the age-old philosophic attempt to discover the first causes and true principles upon which infallible knowledge might be grounded. Some of the information obtained in the other four ways might indeed be of temporary usefulness in the practical conduct of life; but only the new method of rightly conducting the reason offered the sure means for separating the dubitable from the indubitable. Descartes' philosophy was "new" because it was unique in being estab-

18. *Ibid.*, p. 6.   19. *Ibid.*, p. 91.   20. *Ibid.*, pp. 205–6.

lished "on the true principles by which we may arrive at that highest point of wisdom in which the sovereign good of the life of man consists." [21] Descartes' method was thus established absolutely, as were the results it might achieve.

Such a philosophy was "new," therefore, only in one sense of the term. Descartes believed that the eternity of truth was an argument for its antiquity, and his philosophy might consequently be regarded also as the most ancient of philosophies. One proof of the clearness of his principles is "that they have been known from all time, and even received as true and indubitable by all men." [22] The truths of the new philosophy are but "certain primary germs of truth implanted by nature in human minds." [23] In the letter to Father Dinet, in which Descartes discussed the charges of the University of Utrecht that his philosophy was subversive,[24] he wrote:

For, as regards principles, I accept those alone which have been generally accepted by all philosophers, and which for that reason are the most ancient of all; and . . . that which I finally deduce from them appears to be . . . so contained and implied in these principles, that it would seem that it is likewise very ancient, since nature herself has engraved it upon our minds. But, on the other hand, the principles of the ordinary philosophy, at least at the time at which they were invented by Aristotle or by others, were new . . . and nothing has as yet been deduced from them . . . which is not entirely new, since it is every day made afresh.[25]

What is new in Descartes' philosophy is not the discovery of the basic principles from which we may deduce all that we are capable of knowing, but rather, the discovery *that* these principles are the fundamental ones of philosophy.

Although all the truths which I place in my Principles have been known from all time and by all men, nevertheless there has never yet been any one, as far as I know, who has recognized them as the principles from which may be derived a knowledge of all things that are in the world: that is why it here remains to me to prove that they are such.[26]

21. *Ibid.*, p. 208.   22. *Ibid.*, p. 209.   23. *Ibid.*, p. 12.
24. The decree of the University of Utrecht is appended to the letter to Father Dinet. (See Descartes, *Philosophical Works*, II, 345–76, and also Keeling, *Descartes*, pp. 26–27.)
25. Descartes, *Philosophical Works*, II, 359–60.
26. *Ibid.*, I, 209.

The principles of the new philosophy have been engraved on the minds of men since ancient times. They are the oldest of truths. But only Descartes had seen that they provided the foundations for knowledge "of all things that are in the world." The progress of philosophy had awaited the revelation of Descartes. Terrasson's comparison of Descartes to a God who had come down to clear the chaos seems indeed not unnatural.

Descartes himself recognized the fact that his claim to have done what nobody else had done might seem a bit presumptuous, and he attempted to explain how he, alone and without aid from previous thinkers, had come to make the signal discovery of a method allowing one to attain certainty.

Perhaps it may not be thought that the truth will be found in the new philosophy which I promise. For it is not likely that I alone should have seen more clearly than thousands of the most intelligent of men who have accepted the opinions commonly received in the Schools. . . . I reply to this that in truth I make claim to nothing, nor do I profess to see more than other men; but this perhaps has been of use to me, namely, that, not trusting very much to my own genius, I followed only the easiest and simplest roads. For we must not be astonished if anyone makes more progress in following these paths than others, endowed with much greater talent, make over the rough and impenetrable roads which they follow.[27]

But why had not others, "endowed with much greater talent," followed the easiest and simplest roads? The answer may perhaps be found in Descartes' biography. His was essentially a metaphysic of conversion. He reported that the certification of the mathematical method came in his vision of November 10, 1619, when the Angel of Truth appeared to him and authorized his belief that mathematics was the key to truth. In later years Descartes referred to the date on which he had this experience as the decisive moment in which he discovered that he was finally on the correct path. It is this revelation which he wove as an integral part into the metaphysics he began to devise some nine years later. He there took account of the central import of the vision of the Angel of Truth: in the last analysis, the belief that clear and distinct ideas are true and that they apply to external objects is justified through the concurrence of God. We cannot, for example,

27. *Ibid.*, II, 358.

reject the immediate certainty of such a proposition as the *cogito*, but such immediate evidence does not guarantee the validity of science in general. It is only our knowledge of the existence of a God who does not deceive us that can permit us to believe in the possibility of progress in science. In this way the proof that the mathematical method alone led to wisdom depended in the last analysis upon pointing to the existence of God, rather than to the practice of mathematical inquiry itself.

The notion that progress begins *de novo*, with a sort of miracle, is implicit in Descartes. After centuries of darkness Descartes had discovered the primary germs of truth implanted in all minds to be just what they are—the primary germs of truth. And the discovery was not only unprecedented but providential, for Descartes distinguished between the divine intellect and the divine will. In his omnipotence God could have established other laws for nature. He could have made clear and distinct ideas false, unclear and indistinct ones true. He did not do so because he was benevolent. Consequently, the proof of Descartes' essential discovery—that his method is a revolutionary contribution guaranteeing the future progress of mankind in wisdom—rests ultimately on a recognition of God's grace and is not supportable by an acquaintance with God's intellect alone. The revelation of the method owes nothing to past philosophy; and the progress which follows the revelation is a work and a reminder of Providence. In Saint Augustine's words, it is a miracle, an event which "for the admonition of men is . . . thrust in by an unusual changeableness," [28] instructing them in the virtue of following the simplest and easiest paths.

HISTORY AND PROGRESS

Descartes' conception of the relationship of his philosophy to what had gone before set the pattern for a dominant view of Enlightenment thinkers concerning the setting of their own enterprise. The problem involved in the relationship of history to the Cartesian philosophy has been suggested by Jacques Maritain: "If Cartesianism showed itself so savage a ravager of the past in the intelligible order, it is because it

28. St. Augustine, *On the Trinity*, III, 6.

began by disowning in the individual himself the essential intrinsic dependence of our present knowledge on our past." [29]

It is not entirely true, of course, that Descartes thought that knowledge of the past had no function. At the very least, the method employed in the Schools had helped him to discover the uncertainty of everything he had learned.[30] And it had a limited positive function as well. Descartes recognized that a study of the opinions of the past was not entirely useless. "To study the writings of the ancients is right, because it is a great boon for us to be able to make use of the labors of so many men; and we should do so, both in order to discover what they have correctly made out in previous ages, and also that we may inform ourselves as to what in the various sciences is still left for investigation." [31]

There is, however, a special quality in Descartes' views towards the past. What was new in Descartes' philosophy was that the method of systematic doubt had eliminated all the competing and doubtful propositions, leaving the way clear for the systematic use of ancient indubitable principles as the foundation of an infallible philosophy. One might, then, look at the past after the new method had been discovered, but the past would never look the same again. Once the method had been demonstrated it was possible to be *critical* towards the past, to be *modern*. The new method afforded the opportunity for the first time to evaluate received opinions in the light of eternal truths. It was possible to be enlightened, to discover what had been done correctly in the past and what had been left undone. It was possible to study *science* rather than history. "We shall not, . . . though we have mastered all the arguments of Plato and Aristotle, if yet we have not the capacity for passing a solid judgment in these matters, . . . become Philosophers; we should have acquired the knowledge not of a science, but of history." [32]

Significantly, however, the attainment of this capacity was not itself connected with the past. To understand what was worthwhile in the work of past thinkers was not a prerequisite of enlightenment but one consequence of it. Descartes' career as the prophet of the mathematical

29. Maritain, *Three Reformers*, p. 62.
30. Descartes, *Philosophical Works*, I, 317–18.
31. *Ibid.*, pp. 5–6.   32. *Ibid.*

method began with a conversion, and what he had to say about progress reflected the experience of the converted man, of the "twice-born." His past seemed aimless, lost in desire and misplaced hope: it had owned no method for distinguishing the true from the false. The past was the era of mere history; only the present, the period after the revelation, was the era of progress. "Those who have learned least about all that which has hitherto been named philosophy, are the most capable of apprehending the truth. . . . This is diametrically opposite to what I have just said of those who commenced with the ancient philosophy, i.e., that the more they have studied it the less are they fitted rightly to apprehend the truth." [33]

This Cartesian distinction between philosophy and history was passed down to the *philosophes* by such seventeenth-century thinkers as Nicolas de Malebranche and François Fénélon. As Malebranche is reported to have said, "Adam in his earthly paradise knew no history; why should we aspire to know more?" [34] History is concerned with "mere facts"; and erudition, that is, knowledge of particular events, is frivolous so long as it fails to reach the level of clear and distinct ideas or of necessary laws. On the other hand, the discovery of a timeless truth is not a product of historical learning but of philosophical insight; and only after the attainment of true philosophy does the study of history become fruitful. Diderot's remark parallels the sentiments of Descartes: "Some may think that a knowledge of history should precede that of morality: I am not of that opinion: it seems to me more useful and expedient to possess the idea of the just and the unjust before possessing a knowledge of the actions and the men to whom one ought to apply it." [35]

As we shall see, the Cartesian disjunction between philosophy and history tended to become less sharp later in the century. Malebranche's scorn of the historical was balanced by Bayle's use of history as a tool in the struggle for "Reason." But history remained for the eighteenth

33. *Ibid.*, p. 208.

34. This remark is quoted by various authorities, but Gibson, in his *The Philosophy of Descartes*, states that he is unable to find it in Malebranche's works. However, it states Malebranche's position fairly. See, for example, *De la recherche de la vérité*, II, 184 ff.

35. Quoted by Becker, *The Heavenly City*, p. 104.

century primarily *philosophical* history, relatively unconcerned with investigating the specific conditions of individual events, and interested rather in finding in history either illustrations of invariable principles already known or clues that would help in their discovery.

PASCAL AND THE SPHERE OF PROGRESS

Descartes isolated the conclusions of science from the specific mathematical procedures by which they were established by interpreting these conclusions in the light of an external metaphysical theory. In Pascal we find the outstanding example in seventeenth-century France of an alternative way of interpreting science, one resting largely on an appeal to the distinctive nature of scientific method; and suggestively different consequences with respect to notions of progress ensue. Pascal was not without a philosophy that might be called metaphysical and dualistic. But he employed the Cartesian dualism ingeniously. He separated the areas in which experimental methods were exclusively appropriate from other areas in which they had no authority, and then was able to discuss experimental methods separately in their own context without importing alien metaphysical considerations. The Cartesian dualism provided Pascal with the basis for an interpretation of scientific progress exclusively in terms of the character of scientific method.[36]

"I cannot forgive Descartes," wrote Pascal in his *Pensées*. "In his whole philosophy he would have been quite willing to dispense with God. But he had to have Him give a fillip to set the world in motion; beyond this, he had no further need of God."[37] Nevertheless, Pascal's disagreement with the mechanistic implications of Descartes' meta-

36. Pascal's connection with Descartes is complex. In the broad sense that Pascal was also a pioneer in mathematical physics he was a "Cartesian." But his allegiance was to the geometries of Desargues, Cavalieri, and Roberval, rather than to Descartes' analytic geometry. (See Brunschvicg, *Spinoza et ses contemporains*, pp. 311–12.) Furthermore, Pascal thought Descartes' ideal of a deductive physics a "romance," and had little confidence that a mathematical explanation of physical events had other than provisional and experimentally justified grounds.

37. Pascal, *Pensées*, p. 29.

physics (and his suspicion of Descartes' ideal of a deductive physics) did not prevent his recognizing the singular importance of Descartes' revolutionary promulgation of a "new" philosophy. He thought it to have been Descartes' contribution to have dissipated the confusion which caused men to use non-physical terms in investigating physical problems and physical terms in investigating spiritual problems.

Almost all philosophers have confused ideas of things, and speak of material things in spiritual terms, and of spiritual things in material terms. For they say boldly that bodies have a tendency to fall, that they seek after their center, that they fly from destruction, that they fear the void, that they have inclinations, sympathies, antipathies, all of which attributes pertain only to mind. And in speaking of minds, they consider them as in a place, and attribute to them movement from one place to another; and these are qualities which belong only to bodies.[38]

Descartes' work, as Pascal saw it, was to have reinstated the Augustinian dualism of spirit and flesh, mind and body, and to have made it clear (despite Descartes' own excuses) that a divine science must deal with divine things, and a wholly different science with things that are not divine.[39] The Cartesian dualism thus served to demonstrate both the supremacy of revelation and the independence of experimental science from any external authority, so that in Pascal's hands it made possible a non-metaphysical interpretation of science that was radically different from Descartes'.

This position, separating theology from physics and delimiting the appropriate area of each, was developed in the essay which Pascal devoted specifically to the question of progress in science, the *Fragment d'un traité du vide*. One object of the essay was to emphasize the separation of physics from theology: "It is necessary to restore the courage of those timid people who do not dare to invent anything in physics, and to confound the insolence of those impudent persons who bring forth novelties in theology." [40]

The *Fragment d'un traité du vide* grew directly out of Pascal's activities as a physicist. In 1647 he published a study entitled *Nouvelles expériences touchant le vide*. The essay reported the results of Pascal's

38. *Ibid.*, p. 27.   39. See *Pensées*, pp. 86 ff.
40. Pascal, *Œuvres*, II, 133.

investigations into problems that had been raised by Evangelista Torricelli's inquiries into the question of the ascent of liquids. Pascal announced that his work would answer objections like the following: "That this proposition that a space is empty clashes with common sense, and that an imperceptible matter, strange and unknown to all the senses, fills this space." [41] Pascal's work met with immediate objections. The young man seemed to be denying the long-accepted principle that nature abhorred a vacuum. Descartes wrote to Constantin Huyghens: "It seems to me that the young man who has written this paper has a little too much void in his head, and that he is very hasty. I wish the volume he promises had already appeared, so that one might see his arguments, which will be, if I am not mistaken, as unsound as what he has undertaken to prove." [42] A certain Jesuit, Father Noël, was another who took it upon himself to take up the cudgels in defense of the ancient principle that nature abhorred a vacuum. At one time a teacher of Descartes, Father Noël now employed some Cartesian arguments in support of his thesis. He wrote Pascal, arguing that the apparent "void" was really a body of an extremely fine and subtle nature, and that the conception of an empty space was both inconsistent with common sense and self-contradictory, "for all space is necessarily bodily." [43] In support of this argument Father Noël appealed to the nature of light, which, he insisted, could not possibly pass through a vacuum.

The considerations raised by Father Noël led Pascal to more general questions beyond the immediate issue at stake. His reply to Father Noël's letter indicates that he saw the crux of the difference between his opponent and himself to be a fundamental disagreement concerning the issues that are relevant to physical investigations and the criteria that are there to be employed. Pascal's answer involved a consideration of the extent and proper application of the intellectual method which had brought him to such revolutionary conclusions. He attacked Father Noël's arguments for being purely verbal, and irrelevant to experimental procedure. He reproached him for appealing to an entity like light, the nature of which he had neither defined nor

41. Quoted by Brunschvicg, *Pascal*, p. 21. 42. *Ibid.*
43. Pascal, *Œuvres*, II, 87.

was in a position to ascertain. And he went on to express his suspicion that Father Noël's objections came from a misplaced regard for the authority of the ancients.

I know that you can say that you do not stand alone in this matter, and that a number of physicists have already worked it out; but on the subjects relevant to this matter, we do not rest upon authorities: when we cite authors, we cite their proofs, and not their names; we are concerned with the latter only as historical matters. . . .[44]

These statements raise the general issue of the relationship of traditional authority to natural science. How is a method of discovery to be reconciled with respect for tradition? What is the standing of a new discovery founded on experimental evidence, if the appeal to Aristotle, to "common sense," to terms defined outside the context into which they are introduced, or to undefined terms and unknown entities, can singly or together be taken as authoritative? How is the actual continuity of scientific endeavor, illustrated by the growth of Pascal's work out of Torricelli's, to be maintained if such arguments *ab extra* are accepted as relevant? And, on the other hand, how is this very same continuity to be understood if past beliefs are taken to be totally irrelevant to the investigations immediately at hand? Where and in what way is it proper to appeal to authority?

The *Fragment d'un traité du vide,* which was probably contemporaneous with his controversy with Father Noël, contains Pascal's developed ideas on this problem. The opening passage expressed the essay's central purpose: "The respect . . . for antiquity is at such a point today in matters where it ought to have least force . . . that one can no longer advance without peril to novelties, and the text of an author is enough to destroy the strongest arguments." [45] To overcome this obstacle in the way of scientific advance, Pascal distinguished between two kinds of science in terms of the intellectual method appropriate to each. The difference between the two methods is in the differing function that received authority has in each.

There is one class of sciences that is completely dependent upon received authority. History, geography, jurisprudence and, above all, theology, are members of this class. Such sciences cannot go beyond

44. *Ibid.*, p. 97.   45. *Ibid.*, p. 129.

authority, nor can they add to it in any way that is relevant to their proper concerns. The questions they are directed to solve are questions of fact—historic events witnessed in the past, or laws and institutions that have actually been prescribed by some human or divine power. Consequently, such sciences have no other object but to ascertain what is written in the records that have come down from the past. Authority is the sole and sufficient foundation of such sciences: so far as history or theology are concerned, "all that one can know is there contained." [46]

There are other sciences, however, that "fall under the senses or reason." In sciences like mathematics or physics inherited authority is neither the only nor the final court of appeal: it functions through and is modified by experiment and reasoning. "Let us limit this respect we bear towards the ancients. As reason gives birth to it, it ought also to give measure to it." Received authority plays its part in these sciences, but only when it promotes further inquiry. In these sciences authority functions as the point of departure for further discovery rather than as the terminus of investigation. We are truly the pupils of the ancients when we use their knowledge to surpass them, when we can discover new things that it was impossible for them to apprehend. For just as the final appeal of theology is to some authoritative traditional record, the final appeal of experimental science is to experiment. It is precisely this characteristic that makes such science inherently critical and progressive.

The experiments which give us an understanding of nature multiply continually; and, as they are the only principles of physics, their consequences multiply in proportion. It is in this way that one can today hold other views and new opinions than those of the ancients without scorn and without ingratitude, since the initial knowledge that they have given us has served our own to some extent, and since we are thus indebted to them for the superiority we have over them.[47]

Whereas a science like theology is concerned simply to explicate a perfect revelation, physics is concerned "to discover hidden truths," to advance to new facts. Indeed, to fail to add to the physical knowledge the ancients obtained would be to treat the ancients as they themselves did not treat their predecessors. If the ancients had allowed the authorities of their own day to stifle further inquiry in those sciences

46. *Ibid.*, p. 131.   47. *Ibid.*, pp. 132–35.

which are progressive by nature, "they would have deprived themselves and their posterity of the fruit of their inventions. As they did not use those that had been left to them except as means for making new ones . . . we ought to take those that they have left us in the same way, and following their example to make of them the means and not the end of our study, and so to try to surpass them as an imitation of them." [48] The instrument which enables us to surpass them is a method so devised that inherited knowledge is not an end, but a means to experiments that continually accumulate. Progress rests in a method that involves constant criticism of received materials and cumulative discovery.

The capacity to progress, in Pascal's view, distinguishes human intelligence from animal instinct. Human intelligence constantly adds to its possessions whereas instinct always remains in the same state. The animal adapts himself in response to the pressures of the moment, but he forgets just as soon as these pressures have passed. Man is different because he carries his memories with him into the future. "As he conserves his knowledge, he can easily add to it as well." Furthermore, human intelligence is distinctive because it is social. The knowledge gained by any man begins with the knowledge other men have gained in the past, and it becomes in its turn the source of still further inquiries by other men. Man "draws advantages not only from his own experience, but also from that of his predecessors." [49] The sciences that depend on the senses or on reason begin with a social fund of knowledge. And what followed from this insight was of extreme importance: Pascal could urge upon Father Noël adherence to a set of public criteria.

Pascal's interpretation of science was important because it eliminated, at least insofar as natural science alone was concerned, the radical separation established by Descartes between reason and authority, present and past, and even, by implication, between history and philosophy. Pascal retained certain spheres in which authority and the past were inviolate, but, within the practice of science, reason and authority, and present and past, were areas that flowed into one another. "Reason" could not begin without some starting-point, some

48. *Ibid.*, p. 135.   49. *Ibid.*, pp. 138–39.

"authority"; it could not, despite Descartes' attempts to liberate it, be without a past. At the same time, within the method of science, "authority" was not absolute but rectifiable by reason and experiment, and the past was not over and done with, but the constant means to new inquiries. What emerged from Pascal's analysis was the pregnant suggestion that science offered a way of mediating between conflicting claims to authority, and that its actual practice offered a model of a new use and type of authority.

As we shall see, the emerging realization of these revolutionary characteristics of scientific method itself, and of the fact that the claims of scientific conclusions to truth were different from the claims made by other authorities because the meaning of scientific conclusions was not absolute but relative to the specific method which was employed, was to become a significant, though not on the whole a dominant, feature of the *philosophes'* interpretation of the significance of science. Descartes had stressed the singular importance to progress of the new Method, but he had based this Method on external metaphysical grounds. Pascal's argument rested upon distinguishing the characteristic behavior of scientific inquiry from other disciplines in which the function of authority was unchecked; and when his type of argument was stressed, the finished and perfect truth with which progress begins, and the absolute moral goals towards which it moves, fell into the background, and the conception of progress was developed in the light of the actual existence and characteristics of an inherently progressive method.

For Pascal, the fact of scientific method provided the primary impact on his notion of progress. The capacity to progress was due to the possession of a distinctive intellectual technique, and was present only where this technique was in operation. Scientific method was progressive because it was public, cumulative, and self-corrective: its results became the authoritative point of departure for the scientific community, and were to be interpreted in terms of definitions and techniques shared by that community and meaningful in terms of its distinctive practice; and while each of these results was the means to further investigation, it was corrected and enlarged in the very process of inquiry in which it was an ingredient. Pascal's insight was that a conclusion which is offered as absolute, as a final end to all inquiry, and which does not raise further problems, has no place within an indefinitely progressive method. And progress in knowledge was a conditional, not a guaranteed, process which depended on the use of such methods.

> From whence it follows . . . that not only each man advances in the sciences day by day, but that all men together make continual progress in them as the universe grows older. . . . It is in this way that the entire succession of men over the course of so many centuries ought to be considered as a single man who subsists always and learns continually; from whence one sees how unjustly we respect antiquity in philosophers; for as old age is the age most removed from infancy, who does not see that old age in this universal man ought not to be looked for in the times near his birth, but in those which are the farthest from it? Those whom we call ancient were truly new in all things, and were really in the infancy of mankind; and as we have added to their knowledge the experience of the centuries that have followed them, it is in ourselves that one can find this antiquity we revere in others.[50]

THE LIMITS OF PROGRESS

Pascal did, however, set limits to the sphere in which a progressive method could operate. When he wrote the *Fragment d'un traité du vide* he had already come under the influence of Jansenism, and that essay contains suggestions which were more fully developed in the product of his maturer years, the *Pensées*. The *Fragment* wields a double-edged sword. In showing the specific area in which progress takes place, it also cuts off those areas in which progress cannot be made. "The explanation of this difference ought to make us pity the blindness of those who bring only authority for proof in physical mat-

---

50. *Ibid.*, pp. 139–41. This analogy between the life of an individual and the collective career of humanity was widely employed during the seventeenth and eighteenth centuries. Baillet, Descartes' biographer, reports finding a similar passage among Descartes' manuscripts. (See Bouillier, *Histoire de la philosophie cartésienne*, I, 494.) Malebranche used the analogy more than once. See, for example, *De la recherche de la vérité,* Part II, Chapter III. But it is important to see that this analogy was not the premise upon which the proof of progress rested, but rather a conclusion drawn from an interpretation of science, and its meaning was different where science was differently interpreted.

ters, instead of reasoning or experiments, and gives us horror at the malice of others, who use reasoning alone in theology, instead of the authority of Scripture and the Fathers." In the field of theology received authorities do not function as guides to further inquiry but as the final limit of inquiry. "Who will be able to add anything new to what they teach us, since one wants to know only what they contain?" [51]

Although his view of the nature of scientific progress was not controlled by considerations other than the method of science itself, it goes without saying that Pascal's philosophy was not that of a man who was mainly preoccupied with experimental methods. His *Pensées* place scientific progress in a larger moral and spiritual setting, half-skeptical, half-mystical, "a vast sphere, ever drifting in uncertainty, driven from end to end." To take issue here with his general views toward human progress would require that they be torn from the context proper to understand them. But it may be suggested, with reference to the *Fragment* alone, that Pascal went beyond what was required by his separation of faith and reason, and that, while he restored history to a more respectable place, he nevertheless retained the Cartesian division between history and philosophy which prevented history from attaining the status of a progressive science. Pascal seemed to think, for example, that the primacy of revelation *in* religion made it improper to expect progress in our knowledge *about* religion. Certainly, to take another example, history must rest upon available authorities. But no particular authority constitutes a final limit controlling the writing of history. Critical methods may be used to weigh sources against one another, to consider their authenticity and their relative importance. Indeed, received authorities may be used as means to the unearthing of sources hitherto unknown. That we are limited in our knowledge of the past to the sources that have come down from the past is one question; that we may learn something more *about* them and expand our inherited resources through the use of critical techniques is another. Pascal's emphasis upon the ongoing, critical nature of experimental inquiry was a precursor of the later emphasis on the general subversiveness of the new method of philosophy and its fulfillment in "the fermentation of universal reason." But

51. Pascal, *Œuvres,* II, 90.

Pascal confined progress to the natural sciences, and it was the others who later interpreted the development of the new method of philosophy as an event affecting more than our knowledge of the physical world who developed a conception of social progress.

The Experimental Physics of the Soul

> *Locke reduced metaphysics to what it ought to be in fact, the experimental physics of the soul: a kind of physics that is very different from that which deals with bodies. . . . In the latter, one can discover, and one often does discover, unknown phenomena; in the other, facts as ancient as the world exist equally in all men.*
>
> (D'Alembert)

EARLY MANIFESTATIONS OF *"L'ESPRIT PHILOSOPHIQUE"*

THE humanism and skepticism of Renaissance thinkers flowed into the Enlightenment, mingling with Cartesian currents. Michel de Montaigne provided a contrasting conception of the nature and uses of doubting which was extremely influential, and such imposing critics as Pierre Bayle and Denis Diderot looked to him rather than to Descartes as their master. In the seventeenth century Montaigne's spirit of stoic tolerance and disillusion passed into a kind of epicureanism, emphasizing the priority of happiness over salvation, and the inherent worth of human pleasure. Leaning heavily on the writings of Montaigne and Lucretius, it opposed asceticism, sought happiness on materialistic grounds, and trusted man's instincts. The epicurean humanist, Saint-Evrémond, provided a foretaste of the *philosophes'* attempt to divorce ethics from theology and to make happiness the supreme moral standard. Though these seventeenth-century figures did not share the *philosophes'* political interests, they nevertheless anticipated to some extent the utilitarianism of Claude Helvétius and the materialism of Baron D'Holbach.

Strengthening this humanist stream and drawing strength from it were other currents, not limited to France or even to anti-clerical circles. *"Soyez sage,"* was not the maxim of the disenchanted materialist alone. The Jesuits contributed to a theory of happiness that stressed the importance of knowledge in aid of the good life. And long before Voltaire's visit to England, elements of an atomistic and materialistic philosophy had entered France through Holland and the Huguenots. Pierre Coste had translated Locke into French, and Gassendi, the outstanding rival of Descartes during the seventeenth century, with a philosophy stemming from Bacon and, further, from classic epicureanism, influenced not only Locke, but Bayle and Bernard de Fontenelle, and added a more rigorously formulated natural philosophy to the *libertine* tradition.

During the period of the late seventeenth and early eighteenth centuries, when *"l'esprit philosophique"* had its first characteristic manifestations, Bayle and Fontenelle— "the two fathers of modern incredulity," as Joseph de Maistre, some hundred years later, called them —were preëminent among those who began to bring together the interests of humanism and the critical temper of mind associated with the science of which Descartes was the great prophet. Bayle's *Dictionnaire historique et critique* is a prefiguration of the philosophic onslaught upon tradition, and supplied the *philosophes* with some of their most effective critical weapons. Fontenelle applied his antimetaphysical and positivistic skepticism to a wide range of subjects, and, as the historian of the Academy of Sciences, he helped mold a growing public awareness of the importance of science for society.

Bayle and Fontenelle, as we shall see more fully in Chapter VI, were of especial importance in converting the Cartesian attitude towards history into a new form. To a large extent they retained the Cartesian notion that the past was inferior to the present, and the attendant conviction that history could be only a secondary interest for the philosopher. But they placed enlightenment in a historic setting and suggested that progress did not necessarily begin *de novo* with a kind of conversion. There was, as we have seen, among Descartes and his immediate successors something of a sense of a release from the past, a sense that bespoke the excitement of men who had had an unprecedented, but long-awaited, Revelation. The past had best be forgotten; and history, concerned as it is with mere individual details, was not philosophical. But as the eighteenth century moved on it was marked by the rise of philosopher-historians, men like Hume and Edward Gibbon in England, Voltaire, Baron de Montesquieu, and the Abbé Raynal in France, Gotthold Ephraim Lessing and Johann Gottfried von Herder in Germany, who departed from the Cartesian tendency to disparage history as a relatively worthless intellectual venture.

THE TURNING TO BRITISH PHILOSOPHY

To these various influences was joined that of British empiricism. The persistent conflict between British and French mercantile interests during the eighteenth century throws into sharper relief the vigorous intellectual coöperation that went on between the two countries. In a century that began and ended with wars between Britain and France there was an unprecedented process of cross-fertilization in the realm of ideas. Voltaire, Montesquieu, Georges de Buffon, Helvétius, Rousseau, and the Abbé Morellet were some of those who crossed the channel to mingle with British men of letters; David Hume, Horace Walpole, and Edward Gibbon were among those from Britain who were lionized in the *salons* of France.

The French turned to British thinkers for several reasons. Cartesian physics, with its theory of vortices, was moribund. Furthermore, Newton's success accentuated French discontent with the theological and abstractly speculative trend taken by Cartesianism, and his experimental emphasis better suited the growing practical interests of French thinkers. Indeed, to men increasingly interested in political and social issues, and stifled by clerical domination, the secular bent characteristic of the best-known British thinkers was especially congenial; and British success in attaining religious and political liberties made her philosophy seem the natural doctrine for those fighting for religious and political liberties elsewhere. The fact that liberty had a specific location provided indeed a consideration of no small strategic value. Voltaire wrote that he had to disguise at Paris what he could not say too emphatically in London, and one way of discussing liberty without appearing to advocate it was to write a seemingly innocuous account of a foreign philosophy and situation.

It was Locke who provided the philosophical source-book of the Enlightenment. The *philosophes,* positivistic and humanistic as they were, found in Newton more than a successful physicist: they also found a demonstration of the superiority of empirical methods. Newton's work seemed to rest entirely, in Condillac's phrase, on "well-established facts." Locke was regarded as the man who had begun the application of this experimental physics to the human soul and mind. The *philosophes* found a warrant for their positivism in his criticism of abstractions; and their Socratic concern with the human and moral as against the physical found support both in Locke's doubt that physical science could give more than a probable and incomplete account of the external world, and in his contrasting conviction that moral science could be demonstrated with the same degree of certainty as mathematics.

Locke's *Essay concerning Human Understanding* had two qualifications sufficient to commit the *philosophes* to it. Locke made the science of man, at least initially, continuous with physical science; and he made human experience, the human mind, central in understanding either science or nature. In rejecting the Cartesian dualism which permitted mechanistic explanation only in physics, Locke seemed to have laid the foundations for a true science of man by importing the categories of physics into the study of human experience and treating the mind initially as an affair of the impacts of bodies in motion. Locke's reception in France was symptomatic of two things—the attempt to extend scientific inquiry to human affairs, and the central import which human experience held for the *philosophes*. To an age in which it was accepted that the proper study of mankind was man, Locke proclaimed that human experience was the keystone on which everything else in philosophy depended.

But Locke was sufficiently like Descartes so that the advantages of Descartes, the revolutionary, were not completely lost; and even though a new language was used, Cartesianism continued to exert an unmistakable influence. Although he seemed to have altered the

Cartesian dualism by placing man's mind within mechanical nature, Locke did not use the method of science as an index to the nature of human inquiry. Rather, like Descartes, he employed an antecedent view of the human mind to reach conclusions concerning the object and limits of scientific inquiry. This view was based upon the application of principles imported from the science of bodies in motion; but, like Descartes, Locke interpreted the conclusions of natural science as ontologically absolute, isolated from the procedures by which they had been obtained: the external world was composed solely of those primary qualities—motion, figure, extension, number, and solidity—with which physics was concerned.

Furthermore, this approach, like that of Descartes, provided the kind of systematic house-cleaning which, from the point of view of the *philosophes,* was necessary to redirect the human mind along fruitful paths. The differences between Locke and Descartes only made the Cartesian vision that man might begin all over again seem more concrete. Where Descartes had been left with the one indubitable fact of the thinking mind, Locke had worked back to a mind that was like "white paper, void of all characters, without any ideas," a mind subject to an environment that could be controlled in accordance with physical laws. Locke gave the Enlightenment better reason to believe that man could control his destiny, that the mind could be made the creature of a planned environment in which it would conform with the infallible rules of natural morality. His philosophy was the original source of the optimistic determinism of the French Revolution, expressed in St. Lambert's slogan: "Man is an organized and sensitive mass; he receives intelligence from his environment and his needs." [1]

CONDILLAC: THE SHIFT FROM "RATIONALISM" TO "EMPIRICISM"

Among the philosophers who adapted Locke's empiricism to the French situation the most important in developing Locke technically was the Abbé de Condillac. Condillac was regarded as having provided the semi-official formulation of the Encyclopedic program as it

1. Quoted by Windelband, *A History of Philosophy,* p. 522.

bore upon technical philosophic issues. Although Condillac did not devote specific attention to the question of progress, his "empiricist" theory of the origin and development of reason has an obvious bearing upon the idea of progress, and it provided the most immediately influential philosophic context controlling reflection on progress during the Enlightenment. A fairly lengthy consideration of Condillac's technical "empiricism" is necessary here in order to understand the interpretation of science which was fundamental in ideas of progress during the Enlightenment, and in order to see how the Cartesian idea of science, as translated into the language of "empiricism," continued to provide distinguishing features of the *philosophes'* ideas of progress.

The rebellion against Cartesian rationalism, and the adoption of "empiricism" in the tradition of Newton and Locke was often expressed in France as a rejection of the *"esprit de système"* of the seventeenth century, and the substitution of an *"esprit systématique."* The *philosophes* were opposed to systems based upon universal, abstract principles, like those of Descartes, Spinoza and Leibniz. In place of this rationalism they proposed that systems be founded not upon general principles but upon what Condillac called "well-established facts." D'Alembert's statement of the issue was representative: "The art of reducing, as far as possible, a great number of phenomena to a single one which can be regarded as the principle of them . . . constitutes the true *esprit systématique,* which one must be careful not to take for the *esprit de système* with which it does not always coincide." [2]

Condillac's *Traité des systèmes* was the most systematic technical exposition by any of the *philosophes* of their characteristic attitude towards systems.[3] In this work Condillac expressed the empiricist ideal: "In every system there is a first fact, a fact which is the beginning of it, and which, for this reason, is called a *principle:* because *principle* and *beginning* are two words which originally signify the same

2. D'Alembert, *Œuvres,* I, 202.

3. Condillac provided the generally accepted technical basis for the attack on the *esprit de système:* "The taste for systems . . . is today almost entirely banished from good works. One of our best philosophers, the Abbé de Condillac, seems to have given the taste for systems its death-blow." (D'Alembert, *Œuvres,* I, 288.)

thing." In contrast with "hypothetical" systems there is a type of system in which sets of "facts" are so organized that they support and "explain" each other. The ideal system is one in which one fact will explain all the rest. "Well-established facts can alone be the true principles of the sciences." Abstract or hypothetical systems are permissible under certain very limited conditions but they are not permissible in physics, where such conditions cannot be approximated. "Everything . . . in physics consists in explaining facts by facts."[4]

This shift from "rationalism" to "empiricism," from "abstract" principles to particular "facts," also involved the surrender of the Cartesian dream of attaining an absolutely certain or complete system of natural science. "It is to expect too much of the progress of physics to imagine that enough observations will ever be possessed to make a complete system. . . . There will always remain phenomena to discover. . . ."[5]

Nevertheless, despite the real vigor and the apparent plainness of this opposition to Cartesian rationalism, there is a question as to how fundamental the envisaged shift to empiricism was. Descartes conveyed to the French Enlightenment the habit of wholesale doubt, and most eighteenth-century thinkers were indisposed to begin *in medias res*. Such perimetal figures as Buffon and Rousseau begin their works by adopting the methodological device of Descartes (and of Locke as well) : they try to make sure that they are divesting the mind of all its prejudices by initially divesting it of all the ideas imposed upon it by its environment.[6] The *philosophes* took it for granted that inquiry must be based upon an absolute and infallible beginning, one free from special interest or even selective bias, and they consequently perpetuated in their empiricism problems similar to those of Cartesian rationalism.

What the empiricist *philosophes* attempted to do was to substitute unmistakable sensations for indubitable ideas as first principles of inquiry. But this did not release them from the problems we find in Descartes. The Cartesian transcendental doubt persisted in Condillac.

4. Condillac, *Œuvres*, II, 10, 13, 388.   5. *Ibid.*, pp. 334–35.
6. See Buffon, *De la manière d'étudier et de traiter l'histoire naturelle*, in his *Histoire naturelle* (Paris: 1749), and the beginning of Rousseau's *Discourse on Inequality*.

For example, Condillac criticized Descartes for failing to distinguish the psychological sense in which ideas may be clear and distinct from the logical sense, and asserted that his own first principles were psychological. Nevertheless, inquiry still began properly with the indubitable, the clear and distinct: and, fortunately, what was psychologically first was also a logical way to begin. "It is very certain that nothing is more clear and distinct than our perception when we experience sensations." [7] This produced for Condillac, as it did for Locke, the well-known epistemological problem of the existence of the external world. In stripping the mind of all its ideas Locke had been required to account for the initial occurrence of ideas in the empty mind, and to do so he had invoked the prior supposition of an external world of physical bodies in motion. Unfortunately, however, the ideas in our mind, of which all knowledge is composed, provided no empiricist evidence (i.e. no "idea") of the existence of a material something outside our minds. The empiricist was in the position, therefore, of presupposing an external world, but finding that his conclusions and his empirical criteria left him with no basis for believing in such a world. In this situation, Condillac chose to demonstrate the existence of the external world *a priori*.[8] He was of course not alone in doing so, but, as Hume demonstrated, the *a priori* proof of a matter of fact involved the surrender of a consistent empiricist position.

This problem is mentioned briefly simply to show that the shift from "rationalism" to "empiricism" did not succeed in avoiding the epistemological difficulties of Cartesianism. But what is more directly relevant to our present interest is that the attempt to get back to an infallible beginning gave a peculiar cast to Condillac's theory concerning the development and reform of human inquiry. For example:

Because, in our childhood, we think in imitation of others, we adopt all their prejudices: and, when we arrive at the age where we believe we are thinking for ourselves, . . . we only think in accordance with the preju-

7. Condillac, *Œuvres*, I, 495.

8. For example, in his *Logique* Condillac distinguishes between "the evidence of reason," which "consists uniquely in identity," and knowledge of matters of fact, which depends on observation. He then goes on immediately to argue that the evidence of reason demonstrates the existence in fact of a world external to sensation. (*Œuvres*, XXII, 177–80.)

dices that they have given us. Thus, the more the mind appears to make progress, the more it goes astray, and errors accumulate from generation to generation. When things have come to this point, there is only one means for putting order back into thought: that is to forget everything we have learned, to take our ideas back to their origin, to follow the generation of them, and to remake, as Bacon says, the human understanding.[9]

Condillac, like Descartes, thought that progress must begin with a sweeping rejection of received modes of thought, by a return to the valid ingredients of knowledge, available to any man at any time. That these basic elements were simple sensations rather than self-evident principles does not make Condillac's position seem less paradoxical than Descartes'. If a valid idea is one composed exclusively of simple sensations, and if all ideas begin with simple sensations, how does it happen that there are any invalid ideas? To say that improper association of these original elements is the cause of invalid ideas is no answer, because association is a passive response to the environment, and also because analysis—which eliminates invalid associations—is what we are always doing. "To analyze . . . is what nature makes us do at every turn. Analysis, which is believed to be known only by the philosophers, is therefore known to everybody, and I have taught the reader nothing; I have only made him notice what he does continually."[10] If we pick up our bad ideas from other people, where do these other people originally get their ideas? How do we get off to a bad start if only a good start is possible? These questions naturally arise because Condillac's theory of the origin and development of human ideas appears to permit ideas to begin only in valid simple sensations, and accounted for their valid compounding by means of a method we cannot help but employ. In other words, he appeared to guarantee the validity of any idea.

In fact, of course, there was a not wholly explicit distinction between the natural, and the actual, history of the human understanding, and it was a distinction of critical importance in understanding Enlightenment theories of progress. Condillac was proposing that we remake the human understanding by returning to a different beginning from the one which we actually took historically. The peculiar problem which confronted him through all his philosophy was to give an em-

9. Condillac, Œuvres, XXII, 105–7.   10. Ibid., p. 22.

piricist interpretation of norms. Past inquiry had clearly been in error; inquiry could be redirected on sound foundations only if the appropriate norms were employed. But in order to support these norms Condillac felt impelled to show not only that they originate in experience but, like Descartes, to demonstrate that they are always available to the mind of any man any place. In other words, Condillac afflicted his empiricism with the burden of a rationalist ideal of science, and made his normative simple sensations the unchangeable and universal ingredients of any idea. Consequently, just as Descartes found difficulty in squaring the existence of God with the occurrence of vague and unclear ideas, Condillac had the difficult problem of explaining the occurrence of error.

A great deal of the confusion in Condillac's position is eliminated only when we distinguish between two accounts of human inquiry, both of which are present in his analysis. The one is normative and "natural," and lays down the conditions for the development of true ideas; the other is a descriptive account of the growth of error. The first rests on universal principles and does not refer to any specific event; the second describes what has happened and appeals to principles which are not included in the psychology that guarantees that valid ideas will be achieved by the compounding of the simple sensations that come before the mind. Condillac explained why we make errors in terms of one theory. He then proposed that we cure ourselves by reminding ourselves of the other set of principles: we ought to go back and notice what "Nature" teaches us.

Condillac's history of human error leaned heavily in its details on Fontenelle's *Histoire des oracles*. But there was more straining after system in Condillac. To explain the origin of error he appealed to a principle of human nature and to the historical situation in which reflection first began. Men have made errors because they begin to think under the pressure of necessity, where they have to depend on guesses and partial observations. These errors persist after the original pressure is gone. Systems of hypotheses develop because men continue to use the same kind of method that governed man in the earliest stages of inquiry. The existence of hypothetical systems was thus the product of a confusion between the *true* principles or beginnings of a system, and the *actual* principles—the historical beginnings—out of which the system has been developed.

On the other hand, Condillac argued that systems of true ideas are developed by proceeding with sensations as the basis. He criticized hypothetical systems because they did not square with the rule that "all our knowledge comes from the senses," which can only present particular facts. In other words, when Condillac rejected the hypothetical type of system for the fundamental reason that it did not conform to the true order and generation of ideas, he was criticizing this historically derived type of system in the light of another type of system explicitly disengaged from the actual history of inquiry as he saw it. Condillac's criticism of the *esprit de système,* for all his "empiricism," was like Descartes' criticism of scholasticism: he employed criteria which had not been developed historically, but which were "rational," and superior to history, because they were eternally present in all minds.

This dual explanation of the origin of ideas persisted in the Enlightenment and produced a peculiar paradox in theories of progress. Turgot, for example, was aware of the paradox in his maintaining, on the one hand, a belief in progress on the basis of the principle that knowledge grows steadily more adequate as experience accumulates, while, on the other hand, he saw that the history of human opinion was largely the history of error. The paradox was sometimes extremely effective. Voltaire, Holbach, Diderot, and Jeremy Bentham turned to political use what Condillac had developed in a more restricted and specialized context, tracing contemporary institutions back to their origins in custom and usage, and so satisfying themselves that these institutions had no warrant at all. For in the light of their rationalist canons, the fact that something was customary, and had begun merely in history, provided *prima facie* evidence that it was unreasonable. The human understanding was to be remade by following a different path from the one that had been followed historically. Condillac's position was similar. His empiricism served a critical function, his rationalism a constructive one, but these two ingredients of his thought did not interact upon one another. His empiricism was not an instrument of discovery, and his rational principles remained uncriticized.

The Cartesian dualism of *res cogitans* and *res extensa* persisted in the shape of the division between experience and reason.

At most crucial points, indeed, Condillac subordinated his empiricism to his rationalism. In his treatment of moral standards, for example, the paradox so characteristic of Enlightenment thought emerges clearly. As in connection with inquiry, the problem was the status of norms claimed to have the universal validity of rational standards at the same time that they are said to originate in particular experiences. Condillac argued that ideas of morality were traceable to specific sensations—namely, to the perceived conformity of our actions to laws. These laws are empirically "conventions that men have made." Nevertheless, they may be justified by an appeal to Nature rather than to convention.

The laws that determine the morality of our actions are not arbitrary. They are our work, because they are conventions that we have made: however we have not made them alone; nature made them with us, it dictated them to us, and it was not in our power to make others. The needs and faculties of man being given, the laws were also given; and, although we made them, God, who has created us with such needs and such faculties, is, in truth, our only legislator.[11]

This could be interpreted as an argument in favor of accepting any existing law as the inevitable product of human needs and faculties. Being what we are, we can have no real choice about what happens. This was of course not Condillac's intention. Nevertheless, the fact that such an interpretation is possible points to the paradox at the core of Condillac's empiricist criticism of rationalism. Condillac retained the rationalist ideal, and consequently persisted in the separation of history from philosophy, and in formulating moral laws which satisfied the rationalist demand for the universal, the eternal, and the necessary. And similar consequences attended the theory of the progress of human intelligence. The development of inquiry was evaluated in terms of standards that were themselves sanctioned by Nature, which was beyond alteration. The standards invoked to measure progress were thus held to be apart from developing human inquiry, and supplied and supported by a higher authority.

11. *Ibid.,* pp. 56–57.

THE PROGRESS OF LANGUAGE ·

As a natural result of the attempt of the Enlightenment to disengage itself from the supernatural and to lay down a program for human control of human history, there was a marked growth of interest during the eighteenth century in a theory of language. Language is a basic human tool whose presence is perhaps the most pervasive characteristic distinguishing man's social life from other natural events. In a theory of human progress, and especially in a theory that would explain progress as a human achievement, the theory of language held a place not entirely dissimilar from that which the theory of grace held in traditional theology. Among Scottish philosophers language became a subject of major concern; and in France Condillac developed a theory of language that made the study of the progress of the human mind primarily a study of the progress of language. Turgot made much of this approach in his reflections upon progress; we find extensive considerations of language in Rousseau's *Discourse on Inequality;* and Condorcet appends a long discussion of language to the conclusion of his *Progress of the Human Mind.*

Condillac both reflected and reinforced this trend in Enlightenment thought, giving language a place of central importance in the development of the human understanding. Locke's reflections on language seem almost like an afterthought; Condillac, on the other hand, made his own theory of language the distinctive feature of his improvement on Locke. Comparing his work to Locke's at the end of the *Essai sur l'origine des connaissances humaines,* Condillac remarked:

I have tried to do what this philosopher forgot to do; I have gone back to the first operation of the soul, and I have, it seems to me, not only given a complete analysis of the understanding, but I have also discovered the absolute necessity of signs and the principle of the association of ideas.[12]

Condillac considered Locke's contribution to have been the introduction of Newtonian method into the study of man. Condillac attempted to carry Locke's attempt further and to find in the realm of

12. *Ibid.,* I, 502–3.

the mind the same kind of pervasive single principle that he saw as the basis of Newton's physics. The sub-title of Condillac's *Essai* is revealing: *ouvrage où l'on réduit à un seul principe tout ce qui concerne l'entendement.* Newton had brought both celestial and terrestrial phenomena together in terms of the principle of universal gravitation. The whole of physics seemed to rest on a "well-established fact." Condillac proposed to carry Locke's suggestions to the same kind of consummation.

The crucial problem for both Locke and Condillac was to explain the emergence of reflective thought. Dissatisfied with Locke's resolution of the problem, which seemed to him to have departed from a consistent empiricist appeal to observed facts, Condillac had to account for the development of abstract thought (in which the mind is capable of going beyond the present sensation) while retaining the notion of a passive mind. His solution lay in the fact of language. In Condillac's account of the mind language holds the role which the principle of gravitation holds in Newtonian physics. The use of signs is the source of the capacity to recall past sensations at will instead of having to depend on the chance occurrence of sensations. Language allows man to control the contents of his mind. "By the help of signs he can recall at will, he revives, or at least he can often revive, the ideas that are attached to them." [13] Reflection stems from this capacity.

Condillac's theory of language was of critical importance to his philosophy. He believed that it permitted him to account for the development of reflective thought consistently with his empiricist attempt to trace all ideas back to simple sensations in a passive mind. Condillac took great pains to show that language is not the product of a previously existing power of reflection, but that reflective powers are the products of language. He argued that systems of signs are constructed mechanically in the elementary operations of imagination and sensation—that is, originally from sensation. According to Condillac, language began in the instinctive cries and gestures evoked spontaneously by felt needs. These cries, in evoking in other persons sentiments of an analogous kind, were natural signs. When attention was paid to this automatic process of association, the sounds became words, used intentionally to evoke in others the ideas with which they

13. *Ibid.,* p. 86.

were associated. Language was thus developed without the intercession of any mysterious power of thought inaccessible to observation.

Through instinct alone men asked and gave help to one another. I say, "By instinct alone," because reflection could not yet play any part in it. The one did not say, "It is necessary for me to act in such and such a manner in order to make known what I need, and in order to get him to help me," nor the other, "I see by his movements that he wants such and such a thing, I am going to give him possession of it," but both acted in consequence of the need which urged them on.[14]

Once language had been evolved in this way, reflection was possible because words enable us "to consider our ideas separately." In his later works Condillac pursued the suggestion of his *Essai* and argued that "the art of reasoning, reduced to its greatest simplicity, can only be a well-made language." The analytic method of decomposing ideas into the simple sensations of which they consist results in exhibiting the fact that the progress of the understanding is reducible to the progress of language. "True analysis . . . is that which, beginning at the beginning, shows the formation of language in analogy, and in the formation of language the progress of the sciences." [15]

Condillac's account, however rudimentary, and however speculative theories of the origin of language tend to be, is an illustration of his determination to be consistently empiricist, to employ no concept that does not stem from a sensation, and to eliminate occult and unobservable qualities or powers even (and especially) when studying the human mind. To make language the point of departure for a theory of reflective thought has the advantage of placing logical principles in a concretely specifiable context rather than in some super-sensible realm. Nevertheless, Condillac's empiricist account of language retained Cartesian elements that vitiated much of the advantage gained.

Condillac shared with Descartes the belief that the subject-matter of knowledge is such as to lend itself peculiarly and exclusively to analysis of a mathematical kind. This belief governs his theory of the progress of language. In his *Essai sur l'origine des connaissances humaines* Condillac declared himself a Cartesian in the specific sense that he too began with the simplest things. Reflection is a matter of breaking complex ideas down to simple ones, and then rebuilding. "In the art

14. *Ibid.*, p. 262.   15. *Ibid.*, XXII, 167, 151.

of reasoning, as in the art of calculating, all is reduced to compositions and decompositions." Condillac thus carried over into the field of "experience" the conception made fashionable by physics that the alphabet of nature is mathematics alone. In the light of this mathematical ideal he regarded the goal of progress in language as the development of an abstract system of signs, in which calculation would be facilitated as it came to deal increasingly with simple rather than complex notions. He envisaged giving "to all the sciences that exactness which is believed to be the exclusive portion of mathematics." The progress of science thus moves towards the elaboration of a *langue des calculs*. "A more perfect method . . . is only a more simple language, substituted for a more complicated language." [16]

The concept of analogy played a basic part in Condillac's system. Since a well-established fact is in itself singular and particular, it cannot function as a general principle except through the operation of analogy. For example, Newton observes that terrestrial movements may be described in terms of the observed "phenomenon" of gravitation. He then goes on to assert that the same "phenomenon" is the basis of celestial motions. In the case of terrestrial motions, however, he can observe gravitation, according to Condillac, while in the case of celestial movements he can only observe effects similar to those produced by gravitation. In this situation, he reasons by "analogy": since his experience of terrestrial events displays gravitation he infers analogously that the same principle explains celestial events. Analogy thus plays a crucial role in Newton's method, allowing him to establish a system in physics that meets the ideal condition of resting on a single well-established fact. In the last analysis, the formation of language, and consequently the development and progress of the human mind, rests on this operation of analogy. "Analogy: that is what the whole art of reasoning, the whole art of speaking, reduces itself to." [17]

Condillac's notion of analogy was patterned after Newton's *Rules of Reasoning in Philosophy,* and the emphasis he gave to it was anything but unusual. Hume's is a representative statement of what the philosophers of the Enlightenment held to be Newton's basic methodological principle: "It is entirely agreeable to the rules of philos-

16. *Ibid.,* XXIII, 3, 387.   17. *Ibid.,* p. 7.

ophy, and even of common reason; where any principle has been found to have a great force and energy in one instance, to ascribe to it a like energy in all similar instances. This indeed is Newton's chief rule of philosophizing." [18] By "analogy" Condillac referred to the process by which one reasons from a present sensation to one that is absent on the basis of the principle of uniformity.[19]

In short, analogy was "a relation of resemblance," [20] based on the postulate of the uniformity of nature. And since reasoning in the last analysis reduces itself to analogy, this conception has a most important consequence with respect to a theory of language and the progress of understanding. All reasoning is ultimately analytic, and the progress of language is formal and dialectical rather than experimental. The progress of science is the explication of what is contained from the beginning in the simplest kind of calculation with the fingers.

It is analogy that leads us from one language to another, and it leads us only because the new one that we adopt says fundamentally the same thing as the old one for which we substitute it. In the same way it only conducts us from method to method because each is present in the one that precedes it, and because all are present in calculation with the fingers. Therefore in order to discover the new we have only to observe what we have already found.

So the beginning of all the knowledge that we can acquire is in the most common notions.[21]

This view of the progress of science from "the most common notions" thus resembles Descartes' picture of the development of science out of clear and distinct ideas. Condillac's analytic method was concerned to display basic principles (or sensations) which were universally valid, that is, the ultimate ingredients of any possible experience.

18. David Hume, *An Enquiry Concerning the Principles of Morals*, III, 1.

19. "One reasons by analogy when one determines the relation that ought to obtain among the effects by what obtains among the causes, or when one determines the relation that ought to obtain among the causes by that which obtains among the effects." (*Œuvres*, II, 241.) "It is to judge in accordance with the evidence of reason to determine the cause from an effect which can be produced in only one way: when the effect can be produced in several ways, it is to judge them by analogy to say: there it is produced by such and such a cause, so here it should not have been produced by another." (*Œuvres*, VIII, 243.)

20. *Œuvres*, XXIII, 2.   21. *Ibid.*, pp. 230–31.

The meaning of these principles was established retrospectively, by leading them back to their origins in experience. "Insofar as we distinguish different sensations we distinguish kinds of ideas; and these ideas are either actual sensations, or they are only a memory of the sensations that we have had." [22] Consequently, as Condillac argued in *La Langue des calculs* on the basis of his interpretation of "analogy," to invent is only an act of analysis. The analytic method does not lead to new ideas; all new ideas are reducible to those already known—"the most common notions." Condillac developed a picture of a completely formal science developing within the fixed frame of reference set by primitive sensations, identically repeated.

Condillac's empiricism can certainly not be accused of being blind to the fact that formal and analytic reasoning plays a large part in scientific inquiry. But Condillac misconstrued the role it does play, by interpreting it in terms of his prior psychological theory that all ideas are composed of particular sensations supplied to the blank and passive mind by the external world. Consequently, he failed to show the part played by formal reasoning in directing and organizing inquiry into matters of fact as yet unknown. The attendant consequence was of great importance: progress to genuinely new ideas became a matter of chance. The consequences of the separation of Condillac's rationalism from his empiricism, of reason from experience, are exhibited most precisely in his theory of language. On the one hand, progress in the sciences is wholly deductive. On the other hand, discovery—the emergence of genuinely new ideas, not entirely composed of elements previously experienced—must depend on the chance occurrence of new sensations. The conditions for having a genuinely new experience are uncontrollable. Condillac's account of the progress of language and inquiry emphasized the importance of experience, but it was an experience which could not be controlled purposively. Progress towards new ideas depended almost literally upon a "break," upon an intruding and fortunate novelty in the circle of repeating sensations.

22. *Ibid.*, XXII, 25–26.

Philosophy and Physics

All the errors in politics and in morals are founded upon philosophical mistakes, which themselves are connected with physical error. (Condorcet)

PROGRESS, PLEASURE, AND PAIN

CONDILLAC's philosophy provided the generally accepted technical context for philosophic discussion within the Encyclopedic circle. Two related conclusions seemed to follow naturally from his empiricism: (1) the mind was originally a *tabula rasa* and could become whatever the omnipotent environment made it; the human understanding was perfectible once the natural laws of its environment were understood; and (2) the physical world was governed by necessary laws, which extended to human behavior and guaranteed human progress. Theories of progress which gave different weight to one or the other of these notions developed out of Condillac's philosophy. On the whole, Helvétius stressed the first, Holbach the second, the difference being mainly one of emphasis. Each type of theory shared common assumptions with the other, but the differing stress gave a different order of importance to the philosophic arguments and problems involved.

The emphasis upon the omnipotence of environment was associated most clearly with the utilitarian theory for which Helvétius was the outstanding spokesman. Helvétius did not write specifically on progress, but his predominant concern was to show the implications of the advance of science for human happiness, and it was his philosophy

which provided the source for the explicit utilitarian theories of progress developed by Chastellux and others. Helvétius represented the
practical application of Condillac's insistence that all thought has to do
only with elements already given. It is well known that he emphasized
the omnipotence of environment and held the conviction, characteristic of the Enlightenment, that human character was wholly a product of external circumstances. With a well-conceived process of education and an environment reorganized on a rational basis, no limits
could be set to human improvement, for human nature was wholly
malleable. "To be happy and powerful is only a matter of perfecting
the science of education." [1]

The object of education, as Helvétius saw it, was to place a man "in
that situation which will force him to attain the talents and virtues
required in him." [2] And the instrument of the educator was knowledge of the twin sovereigns ruling human nature—the self-interested
pursuit of pleasure and the avoidance of pain. Condillac had emphasized the fact that the teachings of nature amount to the advice "to
avoid that which can harm us, and to seek that which can be useful to
us." [3] Helvétius turned Condillac's emphasis upon the primacy of human needs as the origin and test of value into a principle of social
planning. With knowledge the educator could manipulate the desire
for pleasure and the aversion from pain in such a way as to maximize
the general sum of happiness. Consequently, education could be the
business of the lawmaker as well as the schoolmaster. The wise legislator was one who knew the motives of individuals and was competent
to enlighten their interests.

Being once assured that man always acts in conformity to his interest, the
legislature may assign so many punishments to vice, and so many rewards
to virtue, that every individual will find it in his interest to be virtuous.
. . . Make good laws; they alone will naturally direct the people in the
pursuit of the public advantage, by following the irresistible propensity
they have to their private advantage. . . . It is of little consequence that
men be vicious; it is enough that they be intelligent. . . . Laws do
all. . . .[4]

1. See, for example, Helvétius, *Treatise on Man*, I, 90–105.
2. *Ibid.*, II, 397.
3. Condillac, *Œuvres*, XXII, 98–99.
4. Helvétius, *Treatise on Man*, II, 299–301.

The pivotal importance of Helvétius' utilitarianism in the eighteenth century rested upon its emphasis on the simple, "well-established facts" of man's pursuit of pleasure and avoidance of pain. This greater emphasis on human drives or interests represented the use of one part of Locke's philosophy—that describing the development of ideas out of experience—to destroy the other part of his philosophy which rested on self-evident natural rights. Yet it is probable that Helvétius did not realize how far-reaching the implications of his substitution of utility for natural rights really were. For like other empiricists of the Enlightenment he retained the Cartesian idea that a true science was a body of finished conclusions and the Cartesian ideal of a universal mathematics as the sole alphabet of nature. The accustomed pressure of the intellectual atmosphere made him believe automatically in the utter harmony of nature. Nature was a machine in which every part inevitably fitted, a mathematician's dream in which nothing was wasted, nothing excluded from the grand mathematical equation. And he easily and unconsciously turned this mathematician's dream into a moralist's ideal. A world in which everything fitted mathematically was a world in which nothing was wasted morally. For was not morals after all a branch of mathematics? Helvétius' shift from the language of natural rights to that of pleasure and pain only poorly disguises his overwhelming faith that human society might become essentially like his picture of physical nature, and that each individual might go about his own business and seek his own interest and at the same time promote the general sum of happiness.

Helvétius' utilitarianism borrowed many of its concepts from English theologians. It owed a great deal to the epicurean humanists of the seventeenth century as well, and to the scientific philosophies of Locke and Gassendi. There was perhaps not much that was fundamentally original in what Helvétius did, beyond a sharpening of some of the issues and a more unrelenting consistency in the application of the canon of utility. But it was this very purism and vigor which gave his philosophy its importance. His utilitarianism was overly simple, but its simplicity was an element in its clarity, and it made the relationship between human happiness and science seem unmistakable. Helvétius' philosophy gave impetus to the wave of opinion that brought together humanistic and scientific interests. It provided a simple and forthright argument for the belief that the promotion of happiness was the sole justification of science, and science the only instrument for promoting happiness. Indeed, it did more: it attempted to show that physical science and the science of human affairs were clearly continuous by providing a "scientific" and mathematical measure of happiness. Helvétius' faith—that of the Cartesian *esprit simpliste*—that the ultimate elements to which anything and everything may be reduced are mathematical quantities, suggested the possibility of a calculus of morals based on the assumption that all pleasures are reducible to qualitatively identical units. Pleasures are indistinguishable just as any two physical bodies are ultimately indistinguishable except in terms of their location, their velocity and direction, and their size.

The fundamental weaknesses of Helvétius' philosophy lay in the fact that its utilitarianism was developed within the context of the Cartesian notion of the nature and goal of science. In interpreting science it took its point of departure not from the *method* of science but from an antecedent and metaphysically established notion. It persisted in the Cartesian hypostatization of the conclusions of science apart from the selective methods by which they are reached, so that the objects of mathematical physics became the ultimate entities in nature. The categories by which the physical world was understood provided for Helvétius the only criteria of reality. The consequence was that Helvétius parodied the nature (and diversity) of human happiness by applying physical generalizations broadside to different domains, without taking account of the qualitative differences between these domains. Furthermore, in retaining Descartes' notion that science had an all-embracing goal, and in making "utility" this fixed and supreme goal, he subjected the free practice of science to the confining dictates of a standard external to any particular investigation.

Helvétius went far in attempting to connect "reason" or "science" and human interest, but he succeeded in making the former only the mechanical servant of the latter. He retained the traditional separation between "reason" and "interest," and did not bring the two into more than an external relation to one another. Consequently, he did not emphasize science as an immanent method of behavior, but rather as the external manipulation of individual behavior in the light of indubitable fixed principles. The finished body of science provided a set of external rules, and could guide interests only indirectly, through apt manipulation of other people's pleasures and pains by an enlightened law-giver who knew how to convert private vices into public virtues. In Helvétius' philosophy terms like "reasonable" and "enlightened" refer primarily to actions which conform to certain external canons established by political experts. They do not necessarily imply that the individual who has taken the action has been intellectually deliberate. One reason for the importance of Helvétius was that his philosophy admirably fitted the *philosophes'* political program, enlightened despotism. To most of the *philosophes* political progress took place from the top down, and was the organization of society in the light of principles in the possession of a few enlightened men.

Utilitarianism was employed to develop a theory of progress by the Marquis de Chastellux in his *De la félicité publique*. Chastellux employed the emphasis upon self-interest, and the doctrine of the omnipotence of environment, in order to explain progress, and invoked the utilitarian standard of the greatest happiness of the greatest number in order to measure progress. His book also provided one more instance of the tenuous alliance between utility theory and natural-law theory by retaining the belief of the Physiocrats in the invisible natural hand that brings all things into harmony.

Chastellux's belief in progress grew out of his conviction that the intellectual achievements of his day were a turning-point in human history. He interpreted these achievements, especially in political and social thought, as the disclosure of fixed and invariable principles universally applicable to any society.[5] Something more remained to be done, of course—the deducing of all the implications of these principles, and their concrete application to society. But he believed that mankind in the eighteenth century had recovered its bearings, and that, now under the guidance of sound principles, it would no longer drift aimlessly from error to error. Men would know where they

5. "The investigation of nature, of its fixed, immutable, and necessary laws, would be the first foundation of every doctrine. From these first notions of nature one would pass to its principal products, and then to its limited and individualized actions; *andrology,* or the knowledge of man in general, would serve as the basis of physical and moral medicine, and out of this science would politics be born." (Chastellux, *De la félicité publique,* I, 135.)

wanted to go and how they were to get there. Consequently, the failures of men in the past did not need to be taken as evidence that mankind was irretrievably fallen: the men of the past simply had not had the light. "If men have not yet made great progress in the true politics, no consequence can be drawn from that with respect to the future." [6]

Chastellux's belief that eternal and universal principles of politics had already been discovered governs the way in which he used utility as a measure of human progress. Believing in the omnipotence of environment, he seemed to stress, in opposition to the traditional belief in man's natural corruption, the extraordinary malleability of human nature. But this doctrine was not so radical as it may have seemed. Chastellux was affirming that certain elements in human nature which had been considered unalterable without supernatural aid could be manipulated so as to yield better consequences. The shift to a naturalistic attitude which this doctrine represents was not of minor importance. It placed human nature in a new setting and among new possibilities, and gave weight to certain human qualities which had been disparaged. But it was not so much a shift to the view that human nature was diverse and changing as it was to the belief that certain human characteristics like selfishness, which had traditionally been taken as tokens of man's sinfulness, could be employed on behalf of man's salvation. Beneath the surface of Chastellux's shift in values there persisted the habitual conception that human nature was essentially simple, universal, and constant. Chastellux retained the belief that human nature does not change. Human happiness, any place any time, was reducible to the net sum of pleasures, and the pleasures of all men were qualitatively identical; human nature possessed a fixed complement of needs, and human behavior in any society was completely explicable in terms of immutable and universal natural principles like egoism. It was this idea of human nature that served the utilitarians as the fixed standard by which they measured progress.

For example, Chastellux suggested two questions as a fair test of the relative position of ancient and modern peoples:

"1. How many days in the year, or hours in the day, can a man work without being uncomfortable, without making himself un-

6. Chastellux, *De la félicité publique,* II, 224.

happy? It is recognized at once that this question bears on the nature of the climate, on the constitution and vigor of men, on their education, on their food, etc., all of which can easily be determined.

"2. How many days in the year, or hours in the day, must a man work, in order to procure what is necessary for the conservation and easing of his life?" [7]

Even with all the allowances Chastellux makes for differences in specific conditions like food and climate, it is plain, as Voltaire argued, that these questions cannot easily be answered for all men. Furthermore, as a test of the respective merits of different cultures, they betray the utilitarian tendency to take specific patterns of value for universal models; they suggest that work must be, in any culture, necessarily associated with pain, and the growth of leisure time with progress.

This assumption reveals the deeper influence of the older supernatural idea that the reward for effort comes after the effort is over. When Chastellux talked of pleasure rather than of salvation he simply gave more modern clothing to the traditional, medieval separation of means and ends. Pleasure was the fixed *end,* and the *means* to pleasure were disparaged as servile and painful. Happiness or "comfort" became final products, and the work necessary to gain these ends was not an ingredient of happiness, but merely a device for attaining it. The utilitarian "experimental physics of the soul" consequently provided a moral structure not unlike the structure of the drama of salvation: pain and effort take the place of the vale of tears, and the comfort of passions stilled, interests satisfied, and intelligence at rest, takes the place of the peace that passeth understanding.

This unspoken separation of means and ends became explicit in Chastellux's description of actual human progress. The study of history, Chastellux held, was the retracing of human unhappiness. His besetting problem was, consequently, to explain the paradoxical discontinuity of past and present. How could superstition have been the prerequisite of enlightenment? And if it was not a prerequisite, how could one continue to maintain that there was a lawfulness to history, a necessary order in which events took place, an order which, as we shall see Chastellux believed, guaranteed human progress? Practically

7. *Ibid.,* I, 60.

everything Chastellux has to say about the past makes it difficult to understand how anything at all good could have come out of it. Certainly nothing would seem to be less expected than the wonderful enlightenment of his own day. "If wisdom is the art of living happily," he wrote of the Greeks, "if philosophy is truly the love of wisdom, . . . the Greeks were never philosophers." The Romans, who did not have knowledge of the immutable laws governing mankind, based the laws of nature "on ingenious dreams, and those of society on particular facts." [8] The men who had lived before the Enlightenment had existed in the limbo of desire and misplaced hope.

Chastellux intended his book to provide the answer to this problem by marshalling the historic "evidence" for progress. He claimed, for example, that the devastation caused by war had taught men a lesson, that they were becoming more and more convinced of war's futility, and that the prospects for peace in his time had consequently become much more favorable. The example is illustrative. Chastellux interpreted the historical evidence he called upon in the light of principles he held *a priori* and independently of empirical inquiry. On the grounds of the experimental physics of the soul, of the necessary laws governing the development of the human understanding, Chastellux knew that men necessarily learned from experience, that they knew their interests and could seek them successfully, and that their interests were in harmony with one another.

Chastellux clearly stated two of these principles on which he based his belief in progress. The first was that a man always sought to improve his position; the second was a restatement in different language of the idea that had caught the fancy of seventeenth-century thinkers, that mankind grows wiser through the ages in the way that the adult grows out of the child. Chastellux's restatement of this principle was in the empiricist language of Condillac: the mind was completely under the power of relentless external forces, and built up its ideas out of the sensations presented by an omnipotent environment.

Something else, however, had to be presupposed before these two principles could serve as a basis for a belief in progress. Men might, after all, seek their interests and find them thwarted. The mind might

8. *Ibid.*, pp. 89, 133.

be under the power of external agencies that doomed it to a succession of failures. Chastellux accepted a third principle about which he did not, in his situation, need to be explicit—the metaphysical faith in the harmony of nature. Descartes' Platonic notion that the most real of domains was that clear and distinct world which might be completely formulated mathematically was retained by later Newtonians as the vision of a simple and harmonious Natural Order, in which everything fitted into an intelligible equation. So Chastellux believed that men, in following their drives, were inevitably doing what was best; and he believed that the natural laws that governed the formation of ideas, even if they lead through error, must in the end propel the human understanding inexorably towards truth. For in nature nothing happened in vain:

To subsist and to reproduce is the general law that nature has imposed upon all living beings; and this very simple law is carried out by means that are just as simple: pleasure attaches to all the means of conservation and multiplication; pain is annexed to all the means of destruction. On the basis of this principle, which it is impossible to deny, it is easy to see that the happiness of everything that exists consists uniquely in fulfilling the wish of nature.[9]

Perhaps this was not a teleological argument, nor was an antecedent conscious plan or design affirmed. On the other hand, even if no conscious purpose was involved, nature did have a pattern, and a beneficent one. The argument rested originally on a Spinozistic vision of a universal mathematical fittingness, a systematic aspect in things. But it went much farther and apparently could serve quite satisfactorily (and in very un-Spinozistic fashion) in place of the traditional teleology. For whether it was a justified inference or not, the mathematical structure of things apparently meant to Chastellux that no human interest or experience was wasted, that everything contributed to the improvement of mankind. When Chastellux referred to the "wish of nature," the metaphor was natural. Indeed, it may not have been intended entirely as a metaphor. Progress was the Natural Order as that Order displayed itself in history. Even error and suffering must be factors in progress. "There happened in the moral order what hap-

9. *Ibid.,* II, 237-38.

pens generally enough in the physical order. From the very excess of evil has come the remedy . . ." [10] Chastellux solved the problem of the dissimilarity of the past, the *means,* from the present and future, the *end,* by interpreting the meaning of all past events in the light of principles which had been indubitably demonstrated on metaphysical grounds. These principles could be illustrated by history, but never shaken by it. They remained true even if there were no history, but without them history could not be understood.

Chastellux's theory of progress was strikingly similar to the medieval theory that history was the work of a benevolent Providence. To be sure, Chastellux established worldly objectives for human history. Like Condorcet, he saw progress accomplishing three things: the equalizing of conditions between nations, the equalizing of conditions between individuals, and the real improvement of man. But despite the shift in language from "Revelation" to "Reason," and from "Providence" to "Pleasure," evil and error remained part of a master-plan supporting human strivings. Indeed, Chastellux went very far in order to show not only that error had been the precondition of truth but that the workings of a beneficent nature absolutely required error, just as the design of a benevolent God required that man be free, and so provided the necessary condition for sin.

The concept of man's perfectibility played a similar role in Chastellux's philosophy to that played by free will in the traditional Augustinian philosophy of history. In his utilitarian theory of progress, as in the supernatural theory of Providence, the problem of evil was solved by showing that the prerequisite of man's salvation was also the condition of his fall. Human perfectibility—human egoism plus the inexorable growth of ideas out of experience—was the pivotal concept on which Chastellux's interpretation of history turned. Chastellux argued that man's happiness, like that of other creatures, lay originally in his preserving and reproducing himself. However, just because man was perfectible "he has broken away from this common law, and having soon found it too easy to satisfy his appetites, he has been exposed to boredom and factitious needs." [11] The law of human perfectibility was inexorable. The fact of error did not disprove the law of

10. *Ibid.,* p. 242.   11. *Ibid.,* p. 284.

human perfectibility any more than sin disproves Providence: in both cases they were results of the very perfection of man. And by recognizing his perfection—which now was possible with the revelation of the true principles of scientific politics—and the part it played in the cosmic plan, man could escape the consequences of his fall. "In inquiring whether the perfectibility of men was not the source of their ills, we have found that it was their general remedy." [12]

The similarity extended farther. Chastellux's account of progress resembles the struggle of the heavenly city with those of this earth. Condillac's two accounts of the development of the mind became Chastellux's two histories. The one, normative, natural, and inexorable, revealed the underlying meaning and pattern of history, that is, that "reason always progresses." [13] The other, the story of inherited intellectual sin, revealed the nature of the superstitions that at once bound man and were the prerequisites of man's perfection. When Chastellux argued that "everything that is partakes of what has been," he used the argument morally, to point out man's corruption, and to show that "it is necessary to efface the ancient ideas." [14] The principle that all evil contributes to progress was not a reason for regarding the past as material which the present might use. Once the natural law had been discovered, men can and ought to purge themselves of inherited mistakes. The past had been a means to the present, but was now external to it. Chastellux's was a philosophy of conversion.

What results from all these considerations? that men, in order to be happy, have still more need of forgetting than of learning; that it is necessary, in order to accelerate their progress, to efface, to obliterate, as much as possible, every ancient idea, and to hasten to build the edifice of reason on the ruins of opinion.

In recompense for this sad view of the past, we have felt coming to birth in ourselves a mellow hope for the centuries to come, and a consoling opinion about the present century. We have admired our ancestors less; but we have loved our contemporaries more, and hoped for more from our posterity.[15]

In the last analysis, Chastellux's central problem was simply an inversion of the traditional theological problem of evil. With a super-

12. *Ibid.*, p. 258.   13. *Ibid.*, p. 234.
14. *Ibid.*, pp. 285–86.   15. *Ibid.*, pp. 278, 71.

natural Revelation, the problem was to explain the existence of evil in the light of an omnipotent and benevolent Creator. For Chastellux, Nature was both omnipotent and beneficent; and it was not necessarily a problem that the beneficence of impersonal nature was displayed only gradually and by means of superstition and error. This might simply be the way things worked out. But Chastellux did have to explain how without supernatural aid, men, who partake of what has been, can be expected to turn upon themselves, to reverse the present which partakes of the past, and to "return" to nature.

PROGRESS AND THE LAWS OF MOTION

There were suggestions in Helvétius, and even more clearly in Chastellux, that human progress was implicated in the natural laws governing the motions of all bodies in the universe. And their implicit belief in the harmony of physical nature led them imperceptibly to assume that human history followed a pattern that was both orderly and fortuitously adjusted to human interests. This was the source of Chastellux's recurrent affirmation that the natural development of intellectual and social life was both the source and the cure of evils.

In Holbach's philosophy this conviction played a focal part. "Man . . . is nothing more than a passive instrument in the hands of necessity," [16] but necessity moves man relentlessly forward.

Forbearance, patience, tranquillity, are the effects of an enlightened reason. He who meditates on the things of this world sees them subject to a Nature which, through unforeseen causes and hidden relations, draws concord from discord, happiness even from unhappiness. . . . Let us hope for everything from time and the progress of enlightenment. By dint of falling the child learns to support himself, to walk, to avoid dangers: by suffering from his errors, man becomes wiser and succeeds in curing himself of them.[17]

The notion that mankind, like the individual, grows wiser in time had of course been used in the seventeenth century by many men, usually to attack the too great authority of classic writers, and it had

16. Holbach, *System of Nature,* I, 130.
17. Holbach, *La politique naturelle,* II, 83.

played a part in the development of theories of progress. But not all the men who used the analogy used it in a wholesale way. Pascal and Fontenelle, for example, had stressed its limitations, arguing that it was valid only in the field of science, where a particular method provided the condition for a continuous and critical process of learning from experience. It was, indeed, not this analogy but a conception of the experimental nature of scientific method that had been the basis of Pascal's and Fontenelle's belief in scientific progress. Both of them had been explicit in stating that there was nothing automatic or unconditional about progress, and that men learn from experience only on condition that they possess an appropriate method. Holbach, on the other hand, believing, like Descartes and the long line of Platonists, that what was most certain was also most real, made the conclusions of physics absolute by isolating them from the selective methods by which they had been reached; and from this beginning he took the leap to the categorical position that men were bound to learn from experience. He assumed that sooner or later, after enough misfortunes, men would be compelled to use reason to cure their pains. It does not seem too unfair an analogy to suggest that it were as if repeated blows on the head would in the long run stimulate one's mind.

Holbach took the position that progress was automatic, and misfortune the eventual cause of happiness, on the basis of what he thought was the knowledge imparted by physics. The view that all errors are automatically instructive had already been developed in some detail by Turgot and others. Holbach's contribution to the theory was to emphasize certain "scientific" principles of physics in support of the prevalent belief that men naturally learn in the course of time. Holbach thought that progress would take place as a consequence of man's tendency to advance his own position, and he thought that this human tendency could be inferred from physics. He assumed, further, that man would succeed because nature was harmonious. The principle of inertia, carried over from physics to history and social philosophy, thus became the principle of progress. "Necessity leads men to truth, sooner or later. To struggle against truth is to struggle against the nature of the universe, which compels man to tend towards happiness every moment of his life." [18]

18. Holbach, *Essai sur les préjugés;* quoted by Wickwar, *Holbach,* p. 144.

The cult of Reason and Nature during the Enlightenment was the product of the attempt to divorce the moral ideals of the period from a specific revelation, from a specific history. The cult reached its apotheosis with Holbach's expression of the faith of reason. His radical denial of the Deists' "Supreme Being" prepared the way for his own pantheistic adoration of mechanical law, and his own piety toward nature as the source and fount of human achievement. Holbach inadvertently suggests how much the Enlightenment itself was stimulated by a specific historical incident, which it interpreted as a revelation—that is, the revelation by the sciences of the Order of Nature.

Holbach's faith in progress was side by side with that of Helvétius and Chastellux. In the first place, he shared their attitude towards history. As D'Alembert observed—the same D'Alembert who remarked that it would be a good thing to abolish history—Holbach's political program would be excellent if there were no such thing as history. He had a similar faith in the perfectibility of mankind through education.[19] And he regarded ethics and politics as rigorously deductive, and shared Helvétius' and Chastellux's confidence that the infallible principles of social physics had already been discovered.

The true principles of Government will be clear, evident, demonstrated, for all those who will have reflected upon these important objects; . . . in going back to the nature of man, one can deduce from it a Political System, a harmony of intimately connected truths, a chain of principles as sure as in any of the other branches of human knowledge.[20]

It is extremely important, however, not to mistake the faith of many of the *philosophes* that physical nature supported their ideals for a naïve belief that Utopia was about to be realized. Holbach's rationalistic materialism, for example, was most extreme: in removing an external personal Savior from nature, it simply gave the good cause of the enlightened mind a firmer and more dependable support, releasing it from the fear of the whims or the miracles of a personal deity. But Holbach was not quite the simple-minded and rigorous systematist that some of the romantics made him out to be. He had a

19. "Education is . . . the surest means of inspiring in the people the sentiments, talents, ideas, and virtues which they require." (*La politique naturelle,* II, 125.)

20. Holbach, *La politique naturelle,* I, v.

lively sense of the complexity and diversity of political situations, and he repeated with respect to politics the Aristotelian maxim that not all sciences can expect the same degree of precision: "It would . . . be a ridiculous and frivolous enterprise to pretend to govern all human societies in accordance with uniform laws: it would be folly to prescribe for politics anything but general rules." [21] Nor did Holbach expect a sudden millennium. The extirpation of the spectres of God, freedom, and immortality would, to be sure, remove the principal sources of human ill, but Holbach was convinced that the process of enlightenment was a matter of long effort and constant experimentation. "The perfecting of politics can only be the slow fruit of the experience of centuries." [22]

Holbach's determinism and his emphasis upon the beneficence of nature do not perhaps seem compatible with his reformist program. But, as a practical matter, determinism has not been incompatible with reformist ideals and has often been a powerful philosophy in support of reform. Holbach's materialism was not, after all, primarily a natural philosophy. It was a moral doctrine. He wanted to free men from ecclesiastical domination, and from the other-worldly morality which was the instrument of clerical power. He felt that "a Christian who aims, as he ought, at perfection, is the most useless of members to his country . . . has nothing in common with the interests of this world, and has no more urgent business than to escape from it promptly"; [23] and wanted to displace asceticism as an ideal with a morality aiming at good citizenship. Holbach's philosophy played the traditional anticlerical role of materialistic philosophies. And, after doing away with Providence, it was not without practical effect in this struggle to point to a beneficent Nature, whose guiding hand might lead men progressively towards truth and happiness.

Holbach did not develop a systematic account of progress in terms of the laws governing the motions of physical bodies. In Count Volney's *Les Ruines* the sensationalist account of the development of ideas out of experience and the utilitarian emphasis upon self-love were explicitly placed within the context of physics and made the main-

21. Holbach, *Ethocratie*, II, 109.
22. Holbach, *La politique naturelle*, I, vi.
23. Quoted by Wickwar, *Holbach*, p. 137.

springs of a theory of progress. Volney thought, "Ignorance and the
love of accumulation . . . the two sources of all the plagues that in-
fest the life of man."[24] And conversely, knowledge and enlightened
self-interest were the fundamental factors that made for man's progress.

The disorder his imprudence has caused, his wisdom thus remedied. But
this wisdom was still the effect of the laws of nature in the organization
of his being. It was to secure his own possessions that he was led to respect
those of others, and the desire of accumulation found its corrective in enlightened self-love.[25]

Volney's interest in history was even less than that of Chastellux,
who attempted to produce a great deal of historical "evidence" in addition to his *a priori* arguments. Volney also felt that "the facts of
history" might be so interpreted as to refute any notion of retrogression, but he rested his case even more explicitly than did Chastellux
on the fundamental laws of nature. These moved man towards happiness in the same way that gravitation made stones fall. "The facts
of history might indeed be equivocal, but we should . . . also have to
contradict the living fact of the nature of man; . . . in a word, that
there is no truth in the existing gradation of instruction and experience."

It was as an illustration of a point that had already been demonstrated by the "experimental physics of the soul" that Volney pointed
out that "within the three last centuries especially, the light of knowledge has been increased and disseminated." [26] The dissemination and
popularization of enlightenment was a consequence of the progress of
the human mind in obedience to the laws of nature.

This improvement is the necessary effect of the laws of nature; for, by the
law of sensation, man as invincibly tends to make himself happy as the
flame to ascend, the stone to gravitate, the water to gain its level. . . . By
force of experience he will become enlightened; by force of errors he will
set himself right; he will become wise and good, because it is his interest
to do so.[27]

This law of sensation was part of the physical order of nature. "Man
is governed, like the world of which he forms a part, by natural laws,

24. Volney, *The Ruins*, p. 26.
25. *Ibid.*, p. 28.   26. *Ibid.*, pp. 60–61.   27. *Ibid.*, p. 63.

regular in their operation, consequent in their effects, immutable in their essence; . . . they are at all times and in all places present to the human mind." [28]

Furthermore, Volney made explicit the underlying belief in the beneficent Order of Nature. In his *The Law of Nature* (which carried the significant sub-title, *The Physical Principles of Morals*), Volney attributed a beneficent power to the laws of nature, and, indeed, almost a benevolent intention. Man was, or might be, at home in a universe devoted to his happiness. The law of nature was that "regular and constant order of events, according to which God rules the universe; the order which his wisdom presents to the senses and reason of mankind, to serve them as an equal and general rule of action, and to conduct them, without distinction of country or sect, towards happiness and perfection." [29]

Volney felt he was doing more than simply indicating the effects that would follow *if* certain causes continued to operate. The laws of nature were necessary and could work in no other way than they did. On *a priori* grounds, therefore, every event was necessary for progress. This conception of necessary progress may seem logically to require Volney and Holbach to praise the past because it had been a necessary prerequisite for progress. Indeed, the idea of a ubiquitous natural law relentlessly pushing man forward did result in an attitude different from that of Volney, who would have purged himself of his past. Turgot, for example, used the idea to justify whatever had happened, and emphasized the progressive aspects of the past. Volney's was, however, another possible attitude. The past had been, but it no longer was, a necessary prerequisite for progress. The past, simply because it had already played its role, need no longer be of great concern. Though errors were necessary stages in the progress of knowledge, men had now learned from them, and now no longer needed to remember either the errors or how they had learned. It was a radicalism that met conservative absolutism on its own ground, arguing for the necessity of things, and disagreeing only on what must necessarily pass away. Volney's position might have been paradoxical, but it was no less so than Turgot's: both believed that progress was the steady, in-

28. *Ibid.*, p. 19.   29. Volney, *The Law of Nature*, p. 11.

exorable order of history, and at the same time that the history of the past was a record of folly. It was, as Voltaire discerned, the essential paradox in eighteenth-century optimism: *"Vous criez 'Tout est bien' d'une voix lamentable!"*

The Insane Idea of Becoming
Wholly Reasonable

> *Memnon one day conceived the insane idea of becoming wholly reasonable.* (Voltaire)

PROTESTS AGAINST THE ANALYTIC METHOD

THE *philosophes* were not so doctrinaire and abstract as they have sometimes been held to be. Holbach emphasized that political plans had to be fitted to particular circumstances, Turgot was a public administrator of superior ability, Diderot an editor who knew how to publish dangerous thoughts in relative safety. And it would be difficult to imagine a man more practically successful than Voltaire. The *philosophes* were literary men and reformers, and to a large extent their universal manner and their sweeping generalizations were the techniques of propagandists. Where the intention was to arouse rather than to describe, slogans, paradoxes, and the appeal to universal reason were the natural literary devices.

Yet it is true that there was something vaguely irritating or incomplete about this "philosophic spirit," so universally enlightened, so superior to any convention or to any emotion that was not reasonable. It sometimes seemed too smug, too complete, so unconventional as to be itself merely a fashion, so universal as to belong only to a coterie. Turgot thought the *Encyclopædia* the book of a sect. Rousseau referred to the *coterie Holbachique.*

Criticism of the tight systems developed under the ægis of the analytic method came from within the Encyclopedic circle itself. Rousseau was on the periphery of the circle, and he was not alone in objecting that the principles of the *philosophes* implied a dissection of human sentiments so complete that it would kill them. Diderot, who was the very center of the group, thought the *esprit systématique* of the *philosophes* too close at times to the *esprit de système* they opposed. He feared that the "philosophic spirit" might become rigidly systematic and sectarian, and seemed to sense the fact that the *philosophes,* unlike their great predecessors of the seventeenth century, were a generation living on inherited intellectual wealth, and were in danger of becoming complacent.

ROUSSEAU: THE CRITIQUE OF RATIONALIST PROGRESS

Rousseau has sometimes been regarded as a primitivist opponent of any belief in progress. John Morley, for example, took the view that "the dream of human perfectibility which nerved men like Condorcet, was to Rousseau a sour and fantastic mockery." [1] Professor Bury, in *The Idea of Progress,* has echoed Morley's opinion, maintaining that Rousseau held "a theory of historical Regress." [2]

It is doubtful, however, that Rousseau was so widely removed from the aspirations of his contemporaries. To be sure, his *Discourses* provoked refutations from D'Alembert, Chastellux, and Condorcet on behalf of a belief in progress; and it is true that he did not share their particular conception of progress, which was distinctively generated not only by the attachment to science but by a special conception of the nature of science, and by an attendant conception of "the nature of Nature," both human and non-human. But it is not true that he held no brief for human reason, or that "the dream of human perfectibility was to Rousseau a sour and fantastic mockery."

When Rousseau was attacking a specific institution he usually did so with all the sweeping abstractness of the *coterie Holbachique* which he so much deplored. This universality of manner had the prestige of

1. Morley, *Rousseau,* II, 117–18.
2. Bury, *The Idea of Progress,* p. 177.

sounding like "science," and had the greater force because it gave the impression that what was being attacked was bad in the very nature of things. But it made for certain superficial contradictions which can be over-estimated. Thus, when Rousseau writes that property is the source of all our ills, we are likely to forget that he also thought that property might be a sacred right. His *Discourse on Inequality,* which contains what Professor Vaughan calls Rousseau's "defiant individualism," begins with a dedication to the Republic of Geneva, and ends with an exhortation to men to "respect the sacred bonds of their respective communities." Similarly, the argument in the *Discourse on the Arts and Sciences* can only be conceived as an argument that the arts and sciences are inherently pernicious if we give little weight to the concluding passage of the essay:

Let not princes disdain to admit into their councils those who are most capable of giving them good advice. . . . It is by this means only that we are likely to see what virtue, science and authority can do, when animated by the noblest emulation, and working unanimously for the happiness of mankind.

But so long as power alone is on one side, and knowledge and understanding alone on the other, the learned will seldom make great objects their study, princes will still more rarely do great actions, and the peoples will continue to be, as they are, mean, corrupt and miserable.[3]

The essay that ended on this note was not meant to spread the conviction that the arts and sciences could not contribute to morality. Rousseau was arguing that as a matter of fact they had not, and that this was due to conditions which promoted their abuse rather than their proper use. His concern in the *Discourse on the Arts and Sciences* was to show that in his society responsibility was separated from reason, and political power from political enlightenment. In this respect he was at one with the effort of his Encyclopedist contemporaries to spread enlightenment into affairs of state. Rousseau's distinction lay in his greater emphasis upon the fact that the consequence of the divorce of political power from enlightenment was not only to make political power rest on naked force, but to make "enlightenment" and the arts and sciences frivolous, isolated, and irresponsible. The society which had made obedience to divine right its basic principle had

3. Rousseau, *The Social Contract and Discourses,* p. 153.

smothered genuine feelings of loyalty, and had helped create the philosophy which saw egoism as the only alternative to obedience and
calculation as the only alternative to submitting to infallible authority.
The Encyclopedists were rebellious children of the *ancien régime,* but
they were precisely the kind of children that regime could be expected
to have.

Like the *philosophes,* Rousseau was opposed to a society based on
force, and in which the arts and sciences had no effective function. But
he felt that the philosophies developed through the fashionable "analytic method" were themselves symptoms of the very social conditions
they intended to correct. The social philosophy of the *philosophes*
rested upon the conception of individual rights as developed by Locke,
or, when most consistent, went back to the radical egoism of Hobbes,
in which society was affirmed to rest on force alone.

What is philosophy? What is contained in the writing of the most cele-
brated philosophies? . . . One of them teaches that there is no such
thing as matter, but that everything exists only in representation. Another
declares that there is no other substance than matter, and no other God than
the world itself. A third tells you that there are no such things as virtue
and vice, and that moral good and evil are chimeras; while a fourth in-
forms you that men are only beasts of prey, and may conscientiously de-
vour one another. Why, my great philosophers, do you not reserve these
wise and profitable lessons for your friends and children? You would
soon reap the benefit of them, nor should we be under any apprehension of
our own becoming your disciples.[4]

The arts and sciences had not promoted morality because they had
been isolated philosophically, and separated socially, from the well-
spring of virtue, spontaneous human sentiment. The "analytic
method" simply reflected this isolation by mistaking a part of human
nature, which was the product of social conditions, (e.g., egoism) for
the original whole, and by arbitrarily insisting upon imposing a set of
rationalistic principles on human behavior without respect for human
sentiments like compassion and reverence. In opposition to this morality, Rousseau affirmed that reason could never argue anyone into
having a feeling of obligation. He knew that in his heart he was simple
and affectionate; and he also knew that he was oppressed by other men,
who, he felt, did not share his simple goodness of spirit. So Rousseau

4. *Ibid.,* pp. 150–51.

was convinced that moral obligations could not come from a coldly reasoned decision that saving one's skin or advancing one's condition required one to be just.

> There prevails in modern manners a servile and deceptive conformity. . . . Ceremony has its forms, and fashion its laws, and these we must always follow, never the promptings of our own nature. . . . What happiness would it be for those who live among us, if our external appearance were always a true mirror of our hearts! . . . But virtue rarely appears in so much pomp and state.[5]

It is, of course, Rousseau's emphasis upon the pre-reflective goodness of the "natural man" which has caused many to see in him an enemy of any sort of faith in intelligence, and his attack on the arts and sciences which has been interpreted as that of a sentimental primitivist opposed to the progress of civilized techniques. No less a figure than Voltaire remarked, for example, that Rousseau's two early *Discourses* constituted two attacks upon the human race. And consequently it has seemed to many critics that Rousseau was utterly but characteristically inconsistent in saying in his *Discourse on Inequality* that "a thinking man is a depraved animal," and then going on to argue in *The Social Contract* that "instead of a stupid and unimaginative animal, society made him an intelligent being and a man." But the contradictions are probably more apparent than real. Rousseau himself claimed that "every strong idea in *The Social Contract* had been before published in the Discourse on Inequality," [6] and it is probable that Rousseau's attack upon the excessive rationalism of the *philosophes,* and his conviction that their intellectualistic combination of individualism and cosmopolitanism was the revealing expression of a cold, artificial, and emotionally desiccated society, grew out of the same attitude which led to his emphasis upon emotional individuality and the community.

The problem for Rousseau was not to return to a primitive condition which he expressly recognized to be hypothetical and impracticable. In *Rousseau juge de Jean-Jacques,* the work in which, towards the close of his life, he tried to show the essential unity of his thought, Rousseau repeated his explicit affirmations that "human nature does

5. *Ibid.,* pp. 131, 132.
6. Quoted by Sabine, *History of Political Theory,* p. 580.

not retrogress, and never turns bàck towards the time of innocence and of equality. . . ." [7] To be oneself, "to return to nature," did not mean for Rousseau any more than it did for Condillac to regress historically. Nor did it mean to escape social influences, but only the egoistic, "anti-social" influences of a particular society. The problem for Rousseau was to establish those conditions that would provide outlets for the naturally good instincts of the "natural" man. Convinced of his own spontaneous goodness, Rousseau wanted to inquire into the social and educational conditions which might make it possible for men to be themselves. Rousseau's "natural man" was an ideal in the light of which the misdirected efforts of contemporary society might be detected. Rousseau was an opponent of the continuing progress of the dominant institutions of the *ancien régime* because that progress was really decadence, and because he regarded himself as an apostle of human progress, of the perfectibility of the natural man, when it is rightly understood.

Rousseau's own view of progress, and of the place of intelligence in human improvement, emerges most clearly perhaps in his notion of "nature," which he employed to criticize the doctrines attached to the analytic method. Rousseau attached two meanings to the idea of "nature," but they were not contradictory but rather connected aspects of a single idea. It was only that, in criticizing what was, from his point of view, one or another fallacy, Rousseau employed that particular meaning of "nature" which served as the relevant critical instrument. For Rousseau, "nature" was both the original or "primitive" material with which men must work and out of which they develop, and the fulfilling of the process of which "primitive" nature was the beginning. When men forgot the original drives, capacities, and limitations of human nature, he referred to man's primitive beginnings, as in the *Discourse on the Origin of Inequality*. When men forgot, as, for example, in the individualistic doctrine of "natural rights," the direction in which men must move to be complete, he used the second notion of nature, as in *The Social Contract*. For Rousseau, the natural man was completed in the citizen.

In Rousseau we have the re-emerging conception of nature as a

7. *Rousseau juge de Jean-Jacques;* in Bayet and Albert, *Les écrivains politiques du 18e siècle,* p. 243.

principle of growth, and the foreshadowing of the biological insights which have enriched contemporary psychological and social theory. Rousseau's *Emile* and *The Social Contract* provide a description of the role which reason must play in this larger process of nature: neither of these works places restrictions on "reason," but rather are themselves offered as programs for reason. The one describes the education of a boy bought up to experience the natural and logical consequences of events rather than the frustrations caused by the capricious whims of other persons; the second attempts to show that that society is best in which individuals understand that their best and fullest will is also their most general, social, and rational will.

Reason and science thus had a definite moral function with respect to progress. They were to cultivate those conditions which would be sustained by the natural benevolence of our original sentiments, and which would in turn promote the fuller development of those sentiments. If reason attempted to lay down the law arbitrarily, that is, if it attempted to lead man without regard for his sentiments, or if it was itself without sentiment, then it would corrupt man. But if it was allied to the morality that springs from the heart, it was not only useful, but indispensable, because the heart itself needed guidance. Within a community bound by self-respect and fraternity rather than self-interest, enlightenment and the arts and sciences would be agencies of progress. To conserve them, and to remake them into agencies of genuine progress, it was necessary to attach them to vitalizing sentiments anterior to any art and science. Progress, rightly understood, was for Rousseau the reasonable cultivation of such natural and complementary sentiments as self-respect, sympathy, and conscience. These sentiments provided the initial conditions and possibility of progress, which it was the function of reason to develop.

Rousseau's transcendent importance was to proclaim to an Age of Reason that the moral will, and the passions and emotions, had an essential value without which reason was pernicious. He reminded men that there was more in their experience than was ever dreamt of in their philosophies. But his attack upon the faith in reason was not that of one who opposed intelligence wholesale. He wanted intelligence to fill its proper function—to guide rather than devitalize the emotions. He wanted to make the most popular notions of the En-

lightenment—"the social contract," "natural rights," "liberty"—not
only principles authorized by the mind, but feelings springing from
the heart. What Rousseau proposed was that the sciences and arts recover themselves by recovering a living conscience.

No attempt since Rousseau to apply science to human problems
has been able successfully to avoid taking into account those aspects of
human experience which he stressed. But while his critique of the
narrow categories of rationalism did not logically require him to do
so, Rousseau at times seems to have gone farther than he needed to,
and to have subordinated science to certain antecedent and unanalyzed
sentiments which somehow provided superior insights. It was not
simply that recognition of these sentiments as important subject-
matter for intellectual investigation would enlarge the theory of human nature, nor even that a viable morality would recognize them as
its vital sources, but that these sentiments were themselves a kind of
knowledge, and of a preëminent sort. Even though the idea of human
nature in terms of which he interpreted science was different from
that of Condillac, it was no less an idea that was both external to the
actual practice of human inquiry in science and antecedent to the
scientific examination of human behavior. The "conscience" Rousseau wanted science to recover was in effect his own conscience—one
growing out of antecedently existing sentiments (especially the sentiment of community feeling)—and not the "conscience" which science
itself exhibits in its methodical control of its own practice, and which
might be exhibited in the social use of its conclusions were similar
controls exercised. Rousseau objected to the metaphysics which supported the use of physical generalizations in such a wholesale way as
to divest human experience of its distinctive qualities. But in attempting to reinstate these aspects of human experience, he sometimes
argued as though human sentiments had an absolute cognitive validity which could be maintained without any appeal to rational or
critical analysis. Thus, in place of "the experimental physics of the
soul," Rousseau provided another, and undoubtedly fuller, view of
human nature, but one which was no less external and antecedent to
science. The content of the original Cartesian metaphysics was
changed, but its original impulse and formal structure remained: the

method and role of science were to be understood and justified in the context of larger, extra-scientific truths.

Rousseau's appeal to sentiment was neither wholly a rejection of intelligence, nor the assertion that the arts and sciences were unrelated to progress. But in opposing the reigning metaphysics, Rousseau's own view took on some of its absolutist structure. If Rousseau's conception of human emotions was a good deal more profound than that involved in the calculus of pleasures and pains, it was nevertheless true that the sentiments of which he spoke had the same pristine status protecting them from intellectual criticism or correction as did the simplistic utilitarian conception of pleasure as a fixed, ultimate goal. And where utilitarianism had been motivated by the attempt to extend science to human affairs, Rousseau's faith in the immediate insights of feeling seems at times to have erected those boundaries to the extension of science which his contemporaries had been endeavoring to eliminate.

This aspect of Rousseau's philosophy emerges more clearly when we contrast it with the theories of moral sentiment developed in Scotland by Adam Smith and David Hume. These emphasized that moral obligation had a non-rational element, and denied that reason alone provided moral values. Some interest had to be involved, some sentiment excited. Man was neither so angelically rational, nor so consistently selfish, as to be a good citizen by reason alone. But this was very different from saying that analysis of the emotions was a misleading distortion. Smith and Hume were essentially in accord with the dominant impulse of the Enlightenment towards applying scientific methods to social affairs. Rousseau's frequent massive appeal to sentiment, on the other hand, sometimes tended to take values out of the reach of intellectual analysis, and to put feeling in the same place that had been occupied by the more traditional authorities that had placed restrictions upon the scope of science. It was a position which might lead to the extremes of moral exhortation or moral complacency. And while it was not incompatible with a belief in progress, it made progress an intellectually uncontrollable affair insofar as it insisted that progress would have to begin with feelings which provided in some way insights into truths higher than those of science.

DIDEROT: THE ATTACK ON THE SYSTEMATISTS

If Rousseau's respect for reason has been underestimated, it is also true that his contemporaries' acquaintance with the importance of the passions was underestimated by Rousseau. In 1746, four years before the appearance of Rousseau's *Discourse on the Arts and Sciences,* there appeared a work called *Philosophic Thoughts,* which opened with the remark:

The passions are constantly denounced; all man's troubles are blamed on them, and it is forgotten that they are also the source of all his pleasures. . . . They are never looked at except from the bad side. It is as though one believed he was doing injury to reason to say one word in favor of its rivals; however, only the passions, and the great passions, can lift the soul to great things.[8]

The author of the passage was Denis Diderot, friend of Condillac and, for a while, of Rousseau, and prospective editor of the *Encyclopædia.* If Voltaire was the honorary president of the Encyclopedist circle and Condillac the unofficial treasurer of its intellectual resources, Diderot was the executive secretary, bringing the group together in a common effort, and administering the use of its ideas in varied contexts.

No one was more sensitive than Diderot to the place of the "philosophic spirit" on the contemporary social scene and in history. He saw the practice of free criticism crystallized in the *Encyclopædia,* and regarded this institutionalization of enlightenment as a potent antiseptic against the worst infections of church and state.

In all cases where a national prejudice would seem to deserve respect, the particular article ought to set it respectfully forth. . . . But the edifice of mud ought to be overthrown and an unprofitable heap of dust scattered to the wind, by references to articles in which solid principles serve as a base for the opposite truths. This way of undeceiving men operates promptly on minds of the right stamp, and it operates infallibly and without any troublesome consequences, secretly and without disturbance, on minds of every description.[9]

Moreover, Diderot's *Prospectus* for the *Encyclopædia* suggests that he saw in this organ of liberalism more than a ready-made compen-

8. Diderot, *Œuvres,* I, 127.   9. Quoted by Morley, *Diderot,* I, 143.

dium of information that would disabuse men of their prejudices. It was also an attempt to establish and exhibit the unity of science as a whole, the mutual help given by the individual sciences to one another, and the historic continuity of the scientific enterprise. In this he saw the tableau of the human mind.[10] The *Encyclopædia* was not a finished thing to Diderot but a storehouse of the accumulated learning of history, to be used and enlarged by future generations.

Diderot worked on this Encyclopedic program for many years, but he was never taken in by it. He saw around the problems as did few of his contemporaries, and he raised questions of the most probing kind about materialism, utilitarian morality, and the religion of humanity with its dedication to posterity. If he was a "materialist," he was a materialist of the most distinctive kind. His materialism meant to him the persistent use of scientific methods in all fields, and the conviction that all explanations must be given in terms of the observed behavior of physical bodies. Materialism was for Diderot a philosophy of emancipation, liberating men from teleological explanations, and from the obscurantism of the supernaturalist attempt to use one kind of logic for one kind of affair, and a different kind for another. But Diderot also seemed to be aware, and to fear, that materialism can itself become a kind of crypto-teleology, that it can harden into a new dogma asserting that nature or matter is so constituted as to lend ultimate support to the specific human program which materialists happen to favor. And while he made attempts to speculate about the nature of matter, his very speculations indicate that his materialism was not the belief in a specific theory of matter, but rather the recurrent return to a larger context as a reminder that no human theory is complete, and that no human ideal has the exclusive support of nature. To appeal to matter was a way of preventing systems from becoming rigid, by showing that no distinction between "primary" and "secondary," or between "real" and "unreal," or even between "natural" and "unnatural," was more than a limited human distinction made for specific moral purposes.

Diderot's intellectual life was an adventure in which he moved from deism to atheism and to agnosticism, finding in each a peculiar virtue and in each difficulties of its own. *Rameau's Nephew* explores and dram-

10. See Diderot, *Œuvres*, XIII, 130.

atizes the implications and the paradoxes of a secularized morality; *Philosophic Thoughts on Matter and Motion* exhibits an acute awareness of the limits of the Cartesian view of matter; *D'Alembert's Dream* suggests new and radical views in metaphysics and morals. Diderot did not answer all the questions he raised. One strain stands out in the richly dissonant composition of his thought: he did not like system and would not cut his mind to a pattern. In this respect, the loose and rambling style of his major works was inseparable from what he had to say. It was the relationship he wanted to establish between himself and his reader. His was the "spirit of invention," which "fidgets about in an unruly way." [11]

It is impossible, therefore, to find an "ism" in Diderot which is an adequate representation of his mind. But Diderot's opposition to system-making led him to make radical alterations in accepted theories concerning mind, matter, and science, and it is possible to pick out three separate themes that bear upon the idea of progress: "primitivism," "experimentalism," and "transformism."

DIDEROT'S "PRIMITIVISM"

Diderot's "primitivism" was not a doctrine advocating historical regress. The editor of the *Encyclopædia* did not seriously argue that man was returning or ought to return to an historical period which had once existed. The *Supplement to Bougainville's Voyage,* which Diderot wrote after reading an account of adventures in Tahiti, was his most notable essay on primitivism. In this essay his primitivism was principally a rebellion against the growing complexities and hypocrisies of civilization. It was not offered mainly as an account of what had happened, or even of the direction the future would take, but as an interpretation of what was wrong with the human record. Diderot's "primitivism" was a device for expressing the urge for simplicity which he shared with Rousseau and most of his Encyclopedist colleagues, and it gave a specific content to the notion of simplicity as a reassertion of the claims of natural physiological man against social tabus, and especially against the sacrament of marriage.

11. *Ibid.,* II, 273.

Diderot's emphasis upon the physiological constitution of man carried an unmistakable anarchistic overtone. Diderot inclined "to believe men the more wicked and unhappy the more they are civilized." [12] Civilization brings with it social organization, and the more social organization there is, the more restraints are imposed upon the natural drives of individuals.

If you propose to be his tyrant, then civilize him, persecute him all you are able with a morality contrary to nature; fetter him in all ways; impede his actions with a thousand obstacles. . . . But do you want him to be happy and free? Then don't meddle with his affairs. . . . I appeal to all political, civil, and religious institutions; examine them deeply; and I shall be greatly deceived, if you don't find the human race bowed century after century under the yoke which a handful of scoundrels resolved to put upon it. Beware of anyone who wants to order things. To regulate, is always to make oneself master of the others by hampering them. . . .[13]

Diderot's primitivism dramatized a persistent element in the thought of the *philosophes*—the fact that progress was measured in terms of the increase in individual happiness and that happiness was seen as the release from tensions or frustrations imposed by social organization.

This was of course a significant element in the thought of Helvétius, Rousseau, and others, and it was among the elements that gave the Enlightenment idea of progress its special appropriateness for the economic liberals and the anarchists of the nineteenth century. Diderot's primitivism was a way of emphasizing the notion that social progress was a process of simplification, of becoming, indeed, "less civilized" in the sense in which "civilization" stood for social restraint. But if it was opposed to the arts and sciences which had promoted such organization it was not opposed to those arts and sciences which enlightened people concerning the natural law. Progress was now dependent on such science; and Diderot's primitivism involved neither a turning-back to a simpler time that never was, nor an attack upon art and science in general as unnatural or unprogressive.

Diderot's use of the term "civilization" wavered in his philosophy, accordingly as it was used to represent the advance of complexity and restraint, or the advance of liberating knowledge. Similarly, in the

12. *Diderot, Interpreter of Nature*, p. 189.   13. *Ibid.*, p. 188.

Supplement to Bougainville's Voyage, primitive society represents two contrasting things—on the one hand, it is seen as the lowly and unreasonable origin of the sanctified institutions of "civilized" society; on the other hand, the primitive society of Tahiti is the arch exemplar of natural law in action. Diderot's essay was an allegorical restatement of Condillac's two histories, the one showing the origin of contemporary institutions and beliefs in ancient customs and superstitions, the other recounting man's natural innocence, his fall through his own perfectibility, and his regeneration through the revelation of natural law.

The use of primitive society to show the origin of contemporary institutions was a way of divesting these institutions of their sanctity, of showing the similarity between contemporary behavior and the unenlightened practices of savages. As Diderot used the notion, it was in outline a conception of what we today call "cultural lag." Diderot put this notion to minor use in his essay. From the conditions of primitive life, he argued, "there result different cruel customs, both necessary and bizarre, whose cause is lost in the mists of antiquity, and which put philosophers to the torture to explain them." [14]

This use of the idea of the primitive was, however, distinctly secondary and gave way after the opening passages. One reason behind the interest of the Enlightenment in comparative cultures was that such study loosened the grip of local prejudices and prepared the way for inquiry after a natural and universal morality. But it was more than this alone. The primitive society was also used as an arch exemplar of natural law in action. The example of primitive society was employed in order to silhouette the natural law (or physiological pleasure) in the light of which laws and institutions might be judged. Diderot used the words of the Tahitian as the commentary of nature and reason upon the codes of conduct of European society. Tahiti was not just one society among others; it was, in this essay, the natural society, free (until the coming of the Europeans) from the complexities and obsessions brought about by human meddling and self-interested priestcraft. "I would willingly believe the most primitive people on earth, a Tahitian, who has held scrupulously to the laws of nature, nearer to a good code of laws than any civilized people." [15] It is Orou, the "noble

14. *Ibid.,* p. 150.   15. *Ibid.,* p. 182.

savage," who states "what is good and what is bad in all times and in all places."

Existing primitive societies were employed in the *Supplement to Bougainville's Voyage* as representative of the early stages in the *natural* (that is, ideal) history of human society. There is a rudimentary conception of social evolution in the Supplement, but it is a *natural* evolution, not necessarily an historical one, displaying the laws disclosed by the empiricist account of the development of the understanding and of morals. And there is a great deal of unnatural evolution, which indeed takes up most of the history of Diderot's own civilization.

The life of a savage is simple, and our societies are such complex mechanisms. The Tahitian is at a primary stage in the development of the world, the European is at its old age. The interval separating us is greater than that between the new-born child and the decrepit old man. He understands nothing of our customs, our laws, or he sees in them only fetters which can only excite indignation and hatred in a being for whom liberty is one of the most profound of feelings.[16]

The life of the Tahitian was not, according to Diderot, the very first stage of human society, but a median stage which offered a model of nature. The Tahitians were

wise enough to have stopped themselves of their own accord at a median level of development . . . happy enough to live in a climate where the fertility assures them a long, torpid existence, active enough to provide the necessities of life, and sufficiently indolent for their innocence, repose and happiness to have nothing to fear from a too rapid progress of enlightenment. Nothing was evil there by law or opinion, there was only what was evil in itself.[17]

It was easier for the Tahitian to have a good code of laws because it was easier for him "to get rid of his too-great primitiveness, than it is for us to retrace our steps and remedy our abuses." [18]

Diderot adopted Condillac's account of the origin of error in order to explain the development of society beyond this median level. The pressure of primary needs had given rise to a curiosity that persisted in an uncontrolled way after the needs had been satisfied. "As soon as some physical causes, for example, the necessity for conquering the

16. *Ibid.*, p. 152.   17. *Ibid.*, p. 180.   18. *Ibid.*, p. 182.

barrenness of the soil, have stimulated man's sagacity, this impetus carries him much beyond his immediate objective, and . . . when the period of need has passed, he is carried off into the limitless realm of fantasy, from which there is no coming back." [19]

Thus, much of human history was a digression—a movement away from nature brought on by idle curiosity. "The condensed history of almost all our miseries" is that "there existed a natural man; an artificial man was introduced within this man; and within this cavern a civil war breaks out, which lasts for life." [20] Only sickness or want restore the natural man, and with convalescence he gives way once more to the artificial and moral man. Civilization was a continuous lapsing from the natural. The process could be checked only by the peeling off of the layers of custom that prevent men from observing the natural law, "which we carry always graven in our hearts." [21]

This doctrine of natural primitivism was Diderot's device for disentangling nature from convention, reason from accident. The *Supplement to Bougainville's Voyage* was not a study of Tahiti but of Europe, and by far the greater part of its discussion was concerned not with the effect of primitive society upon a European mind, but with the impact of European society on an observer strange enough to European ways to be able to ask questions about them. The mind of Diderot's "noble savage" was a prism through which might be seen what in European society could be justified by its works and what could not.

DIDEROT'S "EXPERIMENTALISM"

It was not Diderot's primitivism so much as his "experimentalism" and "transformism" that provided a novel critique of the metaphysical categories in terms of which physics had been interpreted and a conception of human progress developed. As we have seen, the analytic method attempted to reduce science to a set of "well-established facts," and was regarded by its proponents as an application of Newton's emphasis upon observation and experiment. In order to destroy the *esprit de système* the "analytic method" worked on the principle that

19. *Ibid.*, p. 181.   20. *Ibid.*, p. 187.   21. *Ibid.*, p. 182.

the human mind was originally a *tabula rasa,* and that human behavior might be explained by tracing the successive imprinting upon the mind of sensations.

The analytic method itself represented an *esprit systématique,* however, and as experimental methods grew increasingly prevalent during the eighteenth century some thinkers turned to the criticism of the mechanistic and materialistic psychology and the geometric analysis that underlay the new sciences of man. Among these figures was Diderot. He was the most philosophically original of the Encyclopedists, and pushed their empiricism to new and radical formulations. More than any of his contemporaries he feared system-making, and he was as sensitive to its effects among the professedly empirical *philosophes* as among the traditional metaphysicians like Descartes. He criticized Helvétius, for example, because *De l'esprit* was too obviously methodical:

Method is a necessary thing in order to work, but it ought not to be apparent after the work is done. It marks a spirit too tranquil, too much master of itself. The spirit of invention asks questions, bestirs itself, fidgets about in an unruly way; it seeks. The spirit of method arranges, orders, and imagines that everything is found out. . . . This is the principal fault of this work.[22]

In contrast with Helvétius, Diderot, significantly, held up for admiration Montesquieu and Buffon, whose work in political theory and in natural history had emphasized the stubbornness with which nature resisted systematic formulation.

Diderot's suspicions of rationalistic empiricism found developed expression in his *Thoughts on the Interpretation of Nature,* the classic eighteenth-century statement concerning the virtues of experimental methods. This work was directed against the "systematists," who did not see things as they were, "but as it would be convenient that they might be. Instead of reshaping conceptions to existing things it seems that one makes a point of modelling existing things after conceptions. Among all philosophers there is none in whom this fury is more evidently dominant than in the systematists." [23]

Diderot was enamored of the practical arts and crafts, and exhibited

22. Diderot, *Œuvres,* II, 273.
23. *Diderot, Interpreter of Nature,* pp. 46–47.

a temper of mind in many ways more attuned to the rising industrial-
ism of England than to the still largely static agrarianism of France.
Furthermore, the actual practice of the scientists was for Diderot more
indicative of an intellectual revolution than philosophies developed
outside the laboratory. Diderot's "experimentalism" was an accom-
paniment to these interests. He was not, of course, a professional laboratory scientist, although his *Letter on the Blind* and his *Elements of
Physiology* indicate that he could be a very acute observer. But to call
his attitude "experimental" is primarily to say that he was impressed
as were few of his colleagues with the complexity of phenomena, with
the subtle individuations that set off one "fact" from another, and
with the consequent danger of the popular method of reasoning by
"analogy." Individual situations were so imperceptibly but significantly different from one another that analogy must naturally tend to
be loose. Impressed with Buffon's emphasis upon the imperceptible
gradations of nature, and upon the arbitrary nature of classification,
Diderot felt that "nature took pleasure in varying the same mecha-
nism in an infinity of different ways. It abandons one kind of produc-
tion only after having multiplied the individuals in it in the greatest
variety of ways." [24] Diderot considered nature as the great Experi-
menter, and his "experimentalism" stood for his attempt to approach
experience without the preconception that it was analyzable into dis-
crete simples, or that it was throughout a mathematically ordered and
intelligible system.

It has been concluded that it was up to experimental philosophy to rectify
the calculations of the geometers; and this consequence has been admitted, even by the geometers. But what good is it to correct geometrical
calculation by experience? Is it not shorter to insist on the result of the
latter? [25]

Diderot carried his conception of experience as an elusive and
changing subject-matter very far, farther indeed than might seem justified. His emphasis upon experimentation was an important counter-
weight to the "systematists," to the ideal of a certain or infallible science, and to the metaphysical belief that those aspects of experience
which were not exactly measurable were unreal or unnatural. And it is

24. Diderot, *Œuvres*, II, 15.   25. *Ibid.*, p. 10.

true that he took account of "reflection" as the mediating stage between observation and experiment. Nevertheless, his "experimentalism" unquestionably involved some depreciation of the function of formal and mathematical disciplines in the development of hypotheses and in the institution and direction of experimentation. In criticizing the belief that mathematics might be made the model for all human knowledge, Diderot even went so far as to prophesy the eventual displacement of the mathematician. "We are on the verge of a great revolution in the sciences. Judging by the penchant that the best minds seem to have for morals, for belles-lettres, for natural history and experimental physics, I should almost be sure that before a hundred years will have passed there will not be three great mathematicians in Europe." [26]

In place of the ideal of scientific certainty associated with mathematics, Diderot set the experimental ideal of detailed and laborious investigation of specific facts.

We have three principal means: the observation of nature, reflection, and experiment. Observation gathers facts, reflection combines them, and experiment verifies the result of the combination. . . . We have distinguished two kinds of science, experimental and rational. . . . Experiment infinitely multiplies its movements; it is always in action; it sets about seeking phenomena all the while that reason looks for analogies. Experimental science knows neither what will come nor what will not come of its work, but it never ceases working. On the other hand rational science weighs possibilities, pronounces judgment, and stops short. It boldly says, "Light cannot be decomposed." Experimental science hears and remains silent for whole centuries, then suddenly displays the prism and says, "Light has been decomposed." [27]

Diderot's experimentalism did not include a thoroughly developed theory of scientific progress or of social progress. Yet, despite its sketchiness and inadequacies, especially with respect to the mathematical and deductive aspects of scientific method, the interpretation of science provided by Diderot's experimentalism was of considerable importance because it rested more directly for its evidence on the actual practise of scientific inquiry, and less upon an antecedent metaphysical theory. The consequence of Diderot's attack upon the "systematists" was to release reflection on progress, insofar as Diderot's

---

26. *Ibid.*, p. 11.   27. *Ibid.*, pp. 18-21.

lead was followed, from the limiting confines of the binding ideology that guaranteed the unprovisional validity of scientific conclusions and certified future success.

Progress itself, for Diderot, thus became an experiment, the future of which was not assured in advance. This view was thus significantly different from that developed under the influence of Cartesian canons. Progress did not rest upon the preliminary establishment of infallible first principles basic to science. The test of hypotheses was rather that they served as conditions for progress, that they opened up new areas for exploration and discovery. "Each experiment that does not extend the law to some new case, or that does not restrain it through some exception, signifies nothing." [28] From the nature of experimental methods it could be predicted that there would be a process of ongoing discovery, but the nature of these discoveries, or the paths that experiment would traverse, could not be guessed in advance. In other words, progress—cumulative and self-correcting discovery—was itself the inherent aim of science: one of the tests of hypotheses was their progressive, ongoing function. In contrast with the view that held that progress in science and society was a consequence of the discovery of absolute truths, Diderot's view suggested that progress was a consequence of the provisional character of scientific conclusions, and, indeed, that the internal progressiveness of the method of science itself provided a new test and index of the status and character of "truth."

DIDEROT'S "TRANSFORMISM"

Diderot's distrust of mathematical analysis was connected with an interest in a type of analysis that might today be called "functional." There is nothing in such analysis that requires the subordination of mathematics, and Diderot's disparagement of mathematics was misplaced except insofar as it corrected general theories of science that drew its ideal exclusively in the image of mathematical certainty. Diderot's "functional" type of analysis expressed his fundamental opposition to the metaphysical position, descended from Descartes, that held that any event could be reduced to ultimate simple ingredients,

28. *Ibid.*, p. 41.

that nothing was lost in such a reduction, and that the distinctive qualities exhibited by bodies as they function in different contexts could thus be explained away as mere illusions. In opposition to this systematist reductionism, Diderot's experimentalism emphasized the specific and distinctive ways in which bodies function on various natural levels. For example, Diderot objected to the categories of "number," "shape," "proportion," and "situation" as limiting and confining: one could not, within such categories alone, account for language, a distinguishing characteristic of human behavior.[29] Diderot was a materialist in the sense that he sought to explain all events as phases in the behavior of physical bodies. But this was not a metaphysical doctrine providing him with a fixed conception of matter that told him *a priori* what the qualities of any event could or could not be. His materialism was simply an emphasis upon the continuity of natural events from one level to another, and the continued applicability of experimental methods once we enter the sphere of human activity.

This "functionalist" emphasis of Diderot's experimentalism was closely related to his marked interest in biology and in speculation concerning the transformation of species. Diderot's opposition to mathematics was related to his biological concerns. On the negative side, these impressed him with the limitations of a metaphysical theory that set a sharp line between man and the rest of nature, or tried to treat men or other animals as merely passive mechanisms. On the positive side, he was impressed with the fact of development, with an unfinished Nature that seemed to be fumbling along from species to species, sometimes creating monsters and sometimes adapted beings, a Nature that seemed anything but the exhibition of a fixed and unchanging plan. Thus, Diderot's experimentalism and his biological interests came together in his "transformism," which emphasized the twin principles of change and of continuity.

29. " 'It is true,' continues the systematist, 'that as a result of my principles of natural history, I have never known how to distinguish man from ape . . . speech is not a distinctive character for me; according to my method, I allow only distinctions which depend on number, shape, proportion and situation.' Therefore your method is bad, says logic. . . ." (*Diderot, Interpreter of Nature,* p. 47.)

Diderot's sense of the pervasive flux and transitoriness of nature set the stage for his critique of the categories of the Newtonian block-universe. Diderot shunned what he called "the sophistry of the ephemeral." "A transient being who believes in the immortality of things," he wrote in *D'Alembert's Dream*, was like "Fontenelle's rose, saying that within the memory of a rose no gardener has been known to die." [30] Any fixed system committed this sophistry, and limited and foreshortened the philosopher's inquiries into the changing nature of things. Such considerations occupy the larger part of the later paragraphs of his *Thoughts on the Interpretation of Nature:*

Just as in the animal and vegetable kingdoms, an individual begins, so to speak, grows, subsists, decays and passes away, could it not be the same with whole species? . . . would not the philosopher, left free to speculate, suspect that animality had from all eternity its particular elements scattered in and mingled with the mass of matter; that it has happened to these elements to reunite, because it was possible for this to be done; that the embryo formed from these elements had passed through an infinity of different organizations and developments . . . that it has perhaps still other developments to undergo, and other increases to take on, which are unknown to us; that it has had or will have a stationary condition; . . . that it will disappear for ever from nature, or rather it will continue to exist in it, but in a form, and with faculties, quite different from those observed in it at this moment of time. [31]

Linked to Diderot's emphasis upon the persistently fluctuating character of natural objects was his conviction that no two individual things were exactly alike and that each thing in nature faded imperceptibly into the next in the chain of being. "Everything is connected in nature, and . . . it is impossible that there should be a missing link in the chain." [32] These twin beliefs in continuity and change led Diderot to attempt to push beyond the confines of the Cartesian dualism. The division of mind from matter, the conception of matter as inert, and the belief that characteristics of events that are lost when the events are reduced to extension and motion are merely appearances, were all results of an inadequate set of categories.

Diderot's dialogues, the *Conversation between D'Alembert and Diderot* and *D'Alembert's Dream,* present the outlines of his "trans-

30. *Diderot, Interpreter of Nature,* p. 75.
31. *Ibid.,* p. 48.   32. *Ibid.,* p. 79.

formism." In the *Conversation between D'Alembert and Diderot,*
Diderot tentatively attacked the Cartesian dualism of mind and body,
and argued that "the faculty of sensation" was a "general property of
matter or a product of its organization."[33] Diderot was aware that the
empirical evidence he employed did not constitute a direct answer to
the question of the specific connection between different natural levels. But he held that such evidence as the life-cycle (whereby inert
matter passes into sensitive matter and then into thinking matter)
furnished at least an initial plausibility to the principle of continuity.
And it was, furthermore, a principle that gave rise to fewer difficulties
than did the dualistic hypothesis.

Diderot's argument that the mind was the function of a particular
kind of material organization involved not only a recasting of the
Cartesian view of mind, but, significantly, a reconsideration as well of
the Cartesian view of matter as wholly inert.[34] Only by affirming that
matter was necessarily inert, Diderot argued, was it necessary to hold
that sensation and mind were incompatible with matter. He attempted
to remove the gap between the human and the non-human by appealing to biological phenomena. In doing so he placed man squarely
among the animals, and, further, forged the conception that matter
was not on all levels mechanical and moved only by external forces.
There was, he argued, living matter as well as dead matter, the difference being one of organization and observable spontaneity of movement.[35] In his *Elements of Physiology,* he went on to say:

> The laws of motion of bodies which are sensitive, animated, organized,
> living, are not even outlined. Anyone who omits from the calculation of
> this last kind of motion, sensitiveness, irritability, life, spontaneity, does
> not know what he is doing. . . .
> Man has all the varieties of existence: inertia, sensitiveness, vegetable
> life, polypous life, animal life, human life.[36]

33. *Ibid.,* p. 59.
34. "This animal . . . walks about, flies, grows angry, runs away, comes
near again, complains, suffers, loves, desires, enjoys. . . . Are you going to
assert with Descartes that it is a purely imitative machine? Little children will
laugh at you, and philosophers will retort that if this be a machine then you,
too, are a machine." (*Diderot, Interpreter of Nature,* p. 58.)
35. See *Diderot, Interpreter of Nature,* pp. 58–59.
36. *Ibid.,* pp. 135–36, 141.

The idea that motion might be internally a character of matter had of course a long history before Diderot. His distinctive interest in the idea was to employ it to support his attack upon Cartesian dualism and the confining metaphysics that established the categories of the physical sciences as the only possible categories for any other science. Diderot developed a rudimentary evolutionary theory and was aware of problems—e.g., emergence—which it raised, although he did not use his revised conception of matter to develop explicitly a new view of progress compatible with the notion that there were no fixed species. His reflections upon the continuity of mind and matter, and upon the transformation of matter from inert to living, did lay the groundwork, however, for a view of human nature different from that developed wholly in terms of the categories of physics. And this had implied consequences for a theory of progress. The mind that figured in progress was not wholly passive, but spontaneous and inventive. Its future operations were not mechanically deducible from its past. And if it was subject to control by external factors, it might also ac- tively change these factors to some extent.

Diderot's transformism also led him to forswear the view of the nature of inquiry that was characteristic among eighteenth-century thinkers. Inquiry could not, and need not, concern itself with the absolute first beginnings or final ends of any process. Diderot thus de- parted to this extent from the regnant ideal of Reason as the knowledge of a few self-evident truths. Progress could not begin *de novo* with the establishment of infallible premises. The principle of transformism rejected this philosophic expedient. Inquiry could be concerned only with specific causes of generation and change.

If you're worried by the question, "which came first, the hen or the egg," it's because you suppose that animals are originally the same as they are now. What madness! We can no more tell what they were originally than what they will become.[37]

In the last analysis, Diderot's transformism supplemented his ex- perimentalism, with its distrust of the analytic method and its central concept, analogy. The principle of transformism, with its emphasis upon the emergence of new levels of organization, was one more

37. *Ibid.,* p. 53.

reason for pointing to the inadequacy of the reductive method of analyzing complex ideas into their simple and qualitatively repeatable
constituents. Convinced of the permanence of change, Diderot did not
look for progress from a method based upon the Cartesian-empiricist
preconception that experience was composed of antecedently fixed
simples, and that ideas were wholly retrospective.

What! don't you see that all the qualities, all the forms by which nature
becomes perceptible to our senses, are essentially indivisible? . . . Acknowledge that division is incompatible with the essence of forms, since it
destroys them. Be a physicist, and acknowledge the produced character of
an effect when you see it produced, even if you cannot explain all the effects that led from the cause to the effect.[38]

Similarly, once it was recognized that nature was a process of the ever-
increasing individuation of matter, it was difficult to place great trust
in reasoning by analogy. "The philosopher . . . must proceed to examine nature, which often shows him a phenomenon quite different
from what he had supposed, and then he perceives that he had been
seduced by analogy." [39]

Diderot's experimentalism and his transformism, more than his
"primitivism," constituted significant deviations from the reigning
ideology of Condillac. These strains do not appear everywhere in Diderot's writings, but his major works show him returning recurrently
to the struggle against the limiting confines of the analytic method. To
this struggle he brought a lively concern with biology, which tempered
his materialism and carried it beyond the mechanistic materialism
dominated by exclusive respect for mathematical physics. In addition,
he saw the danger to the progress of inquiry that was inherent in any
preconception that experience could be completely systematized, or
the extent and end of inquiry laid down in advance. He was aware
that interpreting experience solely in terms of physics might erase
some of the most distinctive qualities of experience, and he used the
traits of living, direct, human experience to provide clues for a more
adequate theory of nature. He was a materialist, but he did not use
matter to explain mind without changing and amplifying his view of
matter in the light of what the inquiry elicited about mind.

These principles provided the opportunity for an ampler view of

38. *Ibid.*, pp. 59–60.   39. *Ibid.*, p. 62.

the conditions and prospects of human advancement. The career of intelligence could be envisaged differently, and the happiness which intelligence might bring no longer had to be interpreted narrowly in terms of the utilitarian conception of an original, unchanging complement of needs. For Diderot anticipated the Lamarckian evolutionary doctrine and argued that needs produce new organs and new organs produce new needs. Whatever the merits of this argument specifically as evolutionary theory, it represented a considerable departure from the belief in a fixed human nature that might serve as an unchangeable standard for measuring progress; and it pointed the way to the problem (and the possibility) of defining progress without invoking fixed and final goals.

VI

The Reign of Reason and Truth

"My daughter," says Reason to Truth, "I think our reign may be just beginning, after our long imprisonment. . . . That will happen to us which has happened to Nature: she has been covered by an ugly veil and completely disfigured during countless centuries. At the end have come a Galileo, a Copernicus, and a Newton, who have shown her nearly naked and who have made men almost amorous of her." (Voltaire)

THE JUNCTURE OF HISTORY AND PHILOSOPHY

THE belief in Reason meant to most thinkers of the Enlightenment that there were a relatively few eternal and self-evident principles intelligible to any man at any time. To discover Reason required no special knowledge or sophistication, only the ability to abstract the essential from what was merely special and habitual. Rousseau expressed the philosophic program when he wrote: "We should distinguish between the variety in human nature and that which is essential to it."

In effect, the Reason which the *philosophes* hoped to find in history was the *essential*—the characters of human nature and morality which were always and everywhere the same. But one possible implication of this project was anything but consonant with the *philosophes'* program. If the nature of the good was unchanging, and if it was written in the hearts of men at any time, one had good reason to believe that other men had been reasonable and to follow obediently in the foot-steps of one's forefathers. Since this was precisely what the *philosophes* did not want to do, seeking Reason meant to them, in effect, seeking the "unhistorical," the essential characteristics of human nature which were hidden and distorted by custom and superstition. Reason was unhistorical—universal not particular, necessary and not contingent upon specific circumstances. When Chastellux or Holbach, for ex-ample, tried to show that Reason worked in history they had to show history as a process of escape from itself, an automatic movement from the unnatural to the natural. In short, the disjunction between Con-dillac's two accounts of human development persisted in the histories that were written by his colleagues. In the case of D'Alembert in par-ticular, it became a clearly stated distinction between a metaphysical explanation of development (involving law) and a merely "historical" explanation (without law) which simply recounted the particular order of succession of particular events. If historical explanation in-volves relating the present to the past in terms of law, and an emphasis upon social influences, the *philosophes'* Reason was not in theory historical. It was, in the first place, not the law which connected the actual past with the present. Contemporary superstitions and bar-barism were the creatures of "accidental" customs. And, as D'Alembert illustrated, the Reason or law that was the unity running through variety was not a social law but the principles controlling the itinerary of what he called the "isolated spirit," which was not meant to be an historical concept.

The pursuit of Reason in history by the philosopher-historians of the Enlightenment thus took place in a dualistic context. Voltaire, Montesquieu, Raynal, did not share the attitude of the seventeenth-century Cartesian, Malebranche, that history was a relatively worth-less intellectual pursuit. But they might turn to history for reasons that were not un-Cartesian: they turned to history to discover un-historical Reason. The principal function of history, according to D'Alembert, was to serve as a warehouse of information about the natural law. History must lead back, in the words of Condillac and so many of the *philosophes,* to fundamental principles, true in all times and places, because they hold to the nature of our heart and of society.

Insofar as the philosopher-historians remained within this context their reflections on progress contained either the paradoxes of Descartes or those involved in the theory of automatic progress associated with Chastellux and Holbach. It was an intellectual context that was well suited to the social situation in which the development of science, the event that stimulated them to reflecting on progress, was taking place, because their dualistic metaphysics eternalized the specific alignment of social science against the seemingly immovable church and state.

But the *philosophes'* sensitivity to the social setting and incidence of the habit of mind represented and stimulated by science, and their consequent interest in the history of enlightenment, was sometimes larger than such a metaphysics theoretically permitted. The histories of the Enlightenment were not entirely dominated by the metaphysics of the isolated spirit, and an interest in history as something more than a mere intellectual grace-note struggled against the confines of the Cartesian ideology. A second tendency, inherited from Bayle and Fontenelle, also influenced attitudes towards history, and, as the century progressed, we can see emerging, tentatively, somewhat unsystematically, but unmistakably, a fuller conception of the importance of cultural and social factors as inescapable conditions of human happiness or unhappiness. From the historians of the Enlightenment came an enlarged conception of the social function of science and a more developed view of social progress.

FONTENELLE: THE HISTORY OF THE NEW METHOD

The first outstanding representative, in the latter part of the seventeenth century, of the interest in history that contrasts with that of Descartes and Malebranche is Bayle. The title of his major work—*Dictionnaire historique et critique*—suggests how Bayle found in history a means for freeing men from their past. Instead of turning away from historical records, Bayle used them as implements in the exposure of time-honored superstitions. In doing so, he appealed to canons of "Reason," but the appeal was different in certain respects from that of Descartes. Bayle's skepticism was closer in nature and intention to Montaigne's; he had a special and insatiable demand for novelty, and was attracted by the richness and variety of details; and, as he employed it, the method of reasonable doubt did not mean the dismissal of history as worthless, but rather getting behind deceptive appearances to the facts of the case.[1]

In Fontenelle we have an interpretation of science which is fundamentally closer to Pascal's than to Descartes', and a significant enlargement thereof by considering the larger relationships of science to history and society. Fontenelle, as his *Eloge de Malebranche* bears witness, could be somewhat ironical about the scorn displayed by Cartesians towards mere memory; and in his *De l'origine des fables* he suggested an alternative to the Cartesian conception that there was a capacity, constant through history and equal among all men, to distinguish the true from the false. Given such a notion, there could be little interest in giving an *historical* explanation of the emergence of the new philosophy, that is, an account of why it should have emerged at a particular place and time. Within the Cartesian philosophy, indeed, as Jacques Maritain has observed, "Whether the poor effort of the individual or the common work of generations is in question, the Cartesian angel only submits to time as to an external compulsion, a force repugnant to his nature."[2] The actual fact of duration itself was, for Descartes, a miracle requiring the perpetual concurrence of God, and he used it as one of the proofs of the existence of God.

Fontenelle, however, did not dismiss the emergence of the new philosophy merely as an individual event, a temporal "accident" which invited no further intellectual concern, but proposed that the new philosophy might perhaps be regarded as a product of the continuous refinement of primitive modes of thought. This was an historical explanation which, in contrast with the Cartesian notion that the new philosophy begins with a sudden revelation possible at any time and place (since the natural light of reason is always present), would account for the emergence of the new philosophy at a specific place

1. See Cassirer, *Die Philosophie der Aufklärung,* p. 271.
2. Maritain, *Three Reformers,* p. 62.

and time. Animating Fontenelle's *De l'origine des fables* and *Histoire des oracles* is the idea of a gradual and continuing release from superstition and animism. This was a notion that permeated the philosophy of history of the Enlightenment and was of special importance to Voltaire. Fontenelle did not entirely discard the Cartesian belief in the constant and universal capacity to distinguish truth from error. But he also suggested as a constant historic factor the continuing cultural process of criticism of which Cartesianism was simply the latest and finest flower. Both these ideas recur in the histories written by the Enlightenment.

Fontenelle wrote specifically on the question of progress in his *Digression on the Ancients and the Moderns*. His argument was in its fundamental respects similar to that of Pascal. It began with the affirmation that "nature holds between her hands a certain stuff that is always the same." [3] Fontenelle made this assertion simply to show that there was no *a priori* reason why the ancients should be superior to the moderns. The ground cleared for his constructive argument, Fontenelle argued that progress actually does take place because human history is distinguished by the fact of communication. But there are types and types of communication, and progress relates to but one type and takes place only in a specific domain. While poetry, for example, is a kind of communication, there is no steady improvement in poetry from age to age. Progress takes place only where communication is controlled by a specific method, for the mere accumulation of ideas in time is not in itself progress: there must also be a method for learning from inherited materials. This critical capacity was provided by the method of science. Sciences like physics and mathematics are progressive because they are concerned with problems of such a kind that the accumulation of many ideas facilitates proceedings, and because they have been put into possession of a unique method that improves with use and makes progress intentional rather than haphazard.

The touchstone of modernity, for Fontenelle, lay in this new manner of reasoning. Before the time of Descartes men had reasoned less rigorously. Descartes' signal contribution was to have introduced in physics and in morals "a precision and accuracy which, until now, had not

3. Fontenelle, *Œuvres*, IV, 236.

been known." This method of reasoning was progressive in that it attained more and more precision and accuracy as it was used. "We shall be ancients some day; and will it not be quite just that our posterity, in its turn, will revise us and surpass us, principally in the manner of reasoning, which is a science apart, and the most difficult and least cultivated of all." [4]

Descartes' emphasis upon the general objective of a method suitable for lighting the way in the various contingencies of life thus passed over into Fontenelle's emphasis upon the profound import of scientific method *qua* method. Fontenelle dealt with method as an historic event, explicable in terms of specific conditions, and developing in time. The distinguishing consequence of this emphasis upon progress in *method* was that progress was interpreted as an ongoing movement in a definite but unlimited direction, rather than a movement towards a final goal. "This constantly growing fund of views to be followed, of rules to be practiced, adds continuously to the difficulty of every kind of science or art; but, on the other hand, new facilities are born that compensate for these difficulties." [5] Fontenelle's originality lay in his repeated emphasis that the scientific method was unique among intellectual disciplines because it could criticize itself, and in his disengagement of *method* as the crucial condition of progress. As Fontenelle wrote, "This new method of reasoning" introduced by Descartes is "very much more estimable than even his philosophy, of which a great part is found false or uncertain according to the very rules he has taught us." [6] Along with Pascal, Fontenelle was a precursor of that element in Enlightenment thought on progress which took its point of departure from an analysis of the new and distinctive character of science as a cumulative and self-rectifying process, rather than from an external idea, borrowed from an antecedent metaphysics, of what the nature and function of science was. The era of the "new philosophy" was distinctive, but not discontinuous with the past. It was distinctive because an organized process of criticism had developed which had control over its own history, making it possible at once to learn from the past and to be liberated from it.

4. *Ibid.*, pp. 242–43.   5. *Ibid.*, p. 249.   6. *Ibid.*, p. 243.

VOLTAIRE: THE STRUGGLE BETWEEN REASON AND SUPERSTITION

Voltaire stamped both the dualism between Reason and history, and the emphasis upon the historical setting and role of intellectual progress, upon the history-writing of his day. His histories were written partly in answer to Bossuet's *Discourse on Universal History*. One of Voltaire's strongest objections to Bossuet's *Discourse on Universal History* was that it was not universal at all, but only a study of a particular and local tradition, making much of the history of Jews and Christians, and subordinating the story of pagan antiquity and other cultures. Voltaire's objection to Bossuet is symptomatic of the attempt of the Enlightenment to disengage its religion and morals from a particular tradition, to make them as universal, natural, and reasonable as Newton's laws of the physical world. Disenchanted with the ancient faiths and unwieldy institutions they inherited, the *philosophes* wished to establish a relationship between God and man, or between sovereign and subject, that was not "accidental," but a logical consequence of the natural order of which man was a part. The abiding purpose behind Voltaire's histories was to disentangle the particular from the universal, the changing from the permanent.

From all that we have observed in this sketch of human history, it follows that whatever concerns human nature is the same from one end of the universe to the other, and that what is dependent upon custom differs, or, if there is any resemblance, it is the effect of chance. The dominion of custom is much more extensive than that of nature, and influences all manners and all usages. It diffuses variety over the face of the universe. Nature establishes unity, and everywhere settles a few invariable principles; the soil is still the same, but culture produces various fruits.[7]

Later in the century a speaker remarked to the revolutionary National Convention: "In dealing with matters so weighty I have sought the truth in the natural order of things and nowhere else. I have descried, so to speak, to preserve the virginity of my thought." [8] But Voltaire had, as it were, to regain the virginity of his thought before he

7. Voltaire, *Works,* IX, 152.
8. Quoted by Sabine, *History of Political Theory,* p. 548.

could begin to preserve it. And he was convinced that this could be done through a knowledge of history. Voltaire was committed to escaping the particular and the provincial, but it was historical knowledge that provided the instrument of liberation from the historical and accidental. History disengaged the natural and reasonable, and revealed the fact and nature of one's provincialism. And because a philosophic understanding of history brought knowledge of the consequences which regularly attended certain actions, the study of history was a phase of morals.

Yet it was a curious phase. For given the abiding principle of Reason, the very fact of history, of development, of change, represented a lapse. Given the lasting capacity of human beings to distinguish the true from the false, their ignorance of the moral law seemed to represent a willful defection. The human need to learn from experience seemed to be a consequence of the vicious traits of man's nature and showed how far man had fallen.

History has kept no account of times of peace and tranquillity; it relates only ravages and disasters. . . . All history . . . is little else than a long succession of useless cruelties, . . . a collection of crimes, follies, and misfortunes, among which we have now and then met with a few virtues, and some happy times. . . . As nature has placed in the heart of man interest, pride, and all the passions, it is no wonder that, during a period of about six centuries, we meet with almost a continual succession of crimes and disasters. If we go back to earlier ages, we shall find them no better.[9]

This curious and recurrent paradox in Enlightenment thought on progress seems all the sharper in Voltaire's case when we remember that he was contending with Bossuet's teleological interpretation of history, and the idea that history was the conflict between Good and Evil, in which the City of God would ultimately triumph. For Voltaire's story was very similar in its outlines. Though he was not concerned to recount the conflict between the City of God and the Kingdom of Satan, history was for him an illustration of the persistent conflict between opposed forces. On the one hand, man was beset by his perennial egoism; on the other hand, his social life developed in fulfillment of his love for social order.[10] Man's "interest," "pride," and "passions" (together with "chance") were the sources of the disasters crowding the pages of history. Yet all the while Reason was time-

9. Voltaire, *Works*, IX, 142, 144, 152.   10. *Ibid.*, pp. 142–52.

less, and man simply grew by experience to become what he was by nature. In Voltaire's transformed history, Reason thus took the place of Super-Nature, Custom the place of Nature, and History became a drama in which "at last, with time, men came to correct their ideas and learn to think." Indeed, in the light of the ubiquity of crime and folly, and the persistence of human egoism and passion, the very triumph of Reason sometimes seems as happily fortuitous as the vouchsafing of God's special Revelation in the traditional Christian epic.

But what may have been a paradox philosophically was an extraordinarily effective dramatic device. Metaphysical dualism is perhaps the natural posture of the moral reformer because it strengthens the distinction between better and worse by making it an eternal division in nature, and exalts the struggle for a specific program into an episode in a cosmic war. Indeed, the very similarity in structure between Voltaire's account and the traditional theological account was an element in its success. By borrowing the force of deep-seated intellectual habits it exerted an immediate appeal to men whose minds were already attuned to looking upon history as a moral drama. In lending a familiar dramatic quality to what was to him the central issue of his time, Voltaire's histories lent it added significance by making it an episode in the central drama of all times. The clash of the *philosophes* with the church acquired a "world-historic" meaning when Voltaire showed that all history was simply a struggle between reason and superstition. Diderot wrote that, where other historians related facts for their own sake, Voltaire's object was to excite hatred of injustice, ignorance, hypocrisy and superstition, and that even after the particular facts had been forgotten the anger aroused by Voltaire's recital remained.[11] The anger remained because, to the philosopher-historian and to his readers, the moral, the *principle* of the thing, was more important than the event.

THE REVOLUTIONS OF THE HUMAN UNDERSTANDING

There was more than the opportunity for righteous indignation, there was the promise of victory, in Voltaire. His histories gave heart

11. See Becker, *The Heavenly City,* p. 92.

to the friends of enlightenment and confounded its enemies by demonstrating that the fruits of superstition and tyranny were all of them ephemeral things as compared with the rarer but more durable works of reason. Writing to a "Professor of History" Voltaire observed that his "principal aim was to trace the revolutions of the human understanding in those of governments." [12] Voltaire's predominant concern was to show that it was through human reason alone that any age left a permanent contribution to those following. Poets and thinkers, rather than kings and politicians, were the true benefactors of the human race. It was with this emphasis that Voltaire brought the tremendous social impact of the intellectual revolution most clearly into the open, and it was his elaboration of this theme that provided the greatest individual impulse to the development of ideas on progress during the Enlightenment. Though he never clearly defined his own conception of progress, it was from him most of all that D'Alembert learned the cultural significance of the development of science; [13] and Condorcet simply developed more systematically Voltaire's central emphasis that the arts and sciences constituted the key to progress. Voltaire was the ancestor of twentieth-century "new historians" concerned to tell the story of "mind in the making."

Voltaire's *Age of Louis XIV* and his *Essays on the Manners and Spirit of Nations* were pioneer works in modern historiography, stressing the cultural context of history rather than its dynastic machinations or wars. The purpose of the *Age of Louis XIV* was to set forth the greatness of the human mind, "the spirit of mankind in general in the most enlightened of all ages." The age of *Le Roi Soleil* was one of the *"quatre âges heureux"* that ultimately merited the historian's attention, ranking with the age of Alexander, the Rome of Cæsar and Augustus, and the Florence of the Medici. Indeed, it outranked them, for "human reason was more improved. In this age we first became acquainted with sound philosophy." [14]

Voltaire's principle of historical selection was frankly moral, as he stated in the *Age of Louis XIV:* "Every transaction is not worthy of being committed to writing. In this history we shall confine ourselves

12. Voltaire, *Works*, XX, 3.
13. See D'Alembert's *Eléments de philosophie,* chapter 2.
14. Voltaire, *Works*, VI, 164 ff.

only to what is deserving of the attention of all ages, what paints the genius and manners of mankind, contributes to instruction, and prompts to the love of virtue, of the arts, and of our country." [15] It was in accordance with this concern that Voltaire placed so much stress upon the work of the intellectual classes, and upon the *quatre âges heureux* in which humanity had made at least some approach to reason. Voltaire's ideas on progress did not develop as did Fontenelle's or Pascal's, out of an examination of the specific nature of scientific method. But the fact of intellectual method and of its context in, and significance for, the manners and character of a people provided the central focus for his views on history. In this respect, Voltaire's emphasis upon the social importance of enlightenment transcended the dualistic ideology of Reason, and provided the stimulus to the interest of other thinkers in progress as an historically denotable fact.

Two ideas mainly governed Voltaire's apprehension of the historic role of enlightenment. Voltaire's histories crystallized the view that the eighteenth century was peculiarly endowed and had a distinctive mission. There was not, Voltaire believed, a single man in Europe whose life had not, in some measure, been affected by the great changes that had swept over Europe during the preceding two centuries and a half. The change was so vast that Voltaire thought that the beginning student of history might well start from the fifteenth century. And the deepest source of this historic revolution was an intellectual movement that had reached its climax in his own century.[16] Voltaire was convinced that "the intellect of Europe has made greater progress in the last hundred years than the whole world has made since the days of Brahma, Fohi, Zoroaster and Thart of the Egyptians." [17]

Secondly, Voltaire was singularly impressed by the continuity in the enterprise of the intellectual classes, and by the durability of their contributions. The works of the mind must in the end constitute the touchstone of an age because they made up in the end most of what remained when the age had passed. Voltaire's belief in progress ultimately rested upon this conviction that the arts and sciences had the greatest power of survival. He was more than aware, for example, of the evils visited upon France by Louis XIV, but he felt nevertheless

15. *Ibid.*, p. 168.   16. *Ibid.*, X, 6–14.
17. Quoted by Torrey, *Voltaire and the Enlightenment*, p. 24.

that these had been outweighed by the tremendous upsurge of French culture during Louis' reign. And because the works of the mind could withstand the onslaughts of time, while those works that were not of the mind must decay, Voltaire looked forward to progress.

The tremendous disasters, which had followed one another in history "almost without a break," would in the long run become less frequent; the works of the mind, the good laws, the monuments produced by the arts and sciences, would last forever. Voltaire did not, of course, expect progress to end in a millennium: men would continue to be men, and calamities would continue to afflict them in all ages. But industry and the art of reason would steadily improve, evils and prejudices would be gradually mitigated, and philosophy, becoming more widespread, would bring men some consolation.

D'ALEMBERT: HISTORY AND METAPHYSICS

In D'Alembert's *Preliminary Discourse* to the *Encyclopædia* Condorcet found one source of his own ideas: "It is a precise tableau of the advance of the sciences since their revival, of their wealth at the time D'Alembert traced their history and of the progress they might still look forward to . . . one of those precious works that two or three men at most in every century are in a position to execute." [18] Condorcet singled out the aspect of the Preliminary Discourse which made it important. D'Alembert, Diderot's chief collaborator, was impressed at every turn with the distinctiveness of his century in its possession of the instruments and the penchant for free inquiry. Voltaire's emphasis upon the cultural setting of progress was echoed by D'Alembert. The *Encyclopædia* in general, and the *Preliminary Discourse* in particular, were imbued with a sense of the historic importance of the scientific revolution, and were devoted to the extension of science to social problems. Quite apart from any metaphysical theory of science or its attendant theory of progress, D'Alembert's *Preliminary Discourse* pointed to the fact of an advancing body of knowledge, indifferent to enshrined authorities and subversive of "tried and true" habits and conventions. Condillac's account of the development of

18. Quoted by Picavet, *Les Idéologues*, p. 105.

ideas out of experience may have provided the theoretical basis for the idea of progress; but what brought the idea to life was the awareness on the part of the *philosophes* of the *fact* of progress within their society.

This social emphasis was obscured and confused in the case of D'Alembert, however, because he did not begin by using scientific practice as a point of departure for understanding the functioning of intelligence. Nor did he look for the laws governing the development of the understanding primarily in actual historic inquiry, or in its cultural context. In accordance with the established metaphysical convention, he offered his interpretation in terms of an antecedent account of the individual mind. There are, indeed, two accounts of the growth of science in the *Preliminary Discourse*. D'Alembert's historical account of the advance of the sciences since their revival is prefaced by "the metaphysical exposition of the origin and connection of the sciences." D'Alembert distinguished this very plainly from "the historic exposition of the order in which our discoveries have succeeded one another." [19] The metaphysical order was explicitly unhistorical in the specific sense that it was unsocial, that it described the order of the generation of ideas as it would take place in an "isolated spirit" not subject to social influence. It was this metaphysical account that served as the basis of the "encyclopedic order" in terms of which the history of science was to be understood. Thus D'Alembert placed the empirically denotable historic progress of the sciences within the context of an ideal and proper order of generation formulated on the basis of antecedent presuppositions about the nature of the mind. The distinction between the two histories of the human mind which was relatively implicit in Condillac became explicit and systematic in D'Alembert, who offers one of the clearest instances of the attempt to apply unhistorical philosophical principles to history, and who reflects the impact of the essentially Cartesian dualism between reason and experience (that is, "normative" and "actual" experience) upon the way in which many thinkers of the Enlightenment looked at their history.

D'Alembert began the *Preliminary Discourse* by pointing out the twofold purpose of the *Encyclopædia*. In addition to being a diction-

19. D'Alembert, *Œuvres*, I, 247–48.

ary of the arts, sciences, and crafts, expounding the basic principles
and content of each, it was also an encyclopædia aiming to exhibit
the order and connection of all human knowledge. A leading principle of the *Encyclopædia* was "to encompass in a single system the
infinitely varied branches of human science." The construction of this
system, D'Alembert maintained, was properly begun by the "return
to the origin and generation of our ideas." [20] This return brought
with it the discovery that all our ideas stem from sensations. The *a
priori* form of the argument in support of this thesis is extremely clear
in D'Alembert's case, and, although he went into considerable "empirical" detail to support it, he held the following argument to be
sufficient: "Nothing is more incontestable than the existence of our
sensations; therefore, in order to prove that they are the principles of
all our knowledge, it is sufficient to demonstrate that they can be." [21]
The argument follows the classic rationalist pattern from possibility
to actuality. On this basis D'Alembert proceeded to give an account of
the development of knowledge from the preliminary stage at which
our sensations teach us of our own existence, through the stage at
which by an "irrepressible inclination," by "a kind of instinct surer
than reason itself," [22] formed in us by our involuntary reception of
sensations, we learn of external bodies, and on through the rise and
development of the sciences and arts.

This empiricist account of the origin of knowledge out of sensations prefaces D'Alembert's presentation of "the encyclopedic tree"
borrowed from Bacon. This encyclopedic tree presents something of a
problem because, after telling us that we find the unity of science by
the empiricist analysis of the origin of ideas, D'Alembert tells us that
the order of the encyclopedic tree, the order and connection of the
various branches of knowledge, is not identical with the true order of
discovery. The encyclopedic tree exhibits the organization of the sciences in graphic form. But it is not a map of the sciences in the order
in which the isolated spirit comes upon them. The encyclopedic order
organizes knowledge in terms of those ideas that are logically first,
whereas the order of discovery is often the order of trial and error, and
always begins with particulars. On the whole, D'Alembert's encyclo-

20. *Ibid.,* p. 185. 21. *Ibid.,* p. 186. 22. *Ibid.,* pp. 187–88.

pedic order appears to correspond closely to what Condillac called "the order of review." Exactly what is meant, however, by the distinction between ideas that are "logically" first, and the atomic sensations that are "first" in the order and generation of true ideas, is not very clear. If the trunk that holds the encyclopedic tree of knowledge together is the human mind, can there be a permissible distinction, in D'Alembert's terms, between the "encyclopedic" order and the "metaphysical" order? And if there is, what is it? D'Alembert himself made an explicit and not altogether satisfactory compromise at this point. He confessed that many principles of organization had presented themselves, and that he had chosen "a division that has appeared . . . to satisfy at once, and as much as possible, the encyclopedic order of our knowledge and their genealogic order." [23]

But whatever its obscurities, the central purpose of the encyclopedic tree is not obscure. As drawn up, the encyclopedic tree epitomized the humanist orientation of the *Encyclopædia*. The proper study of mankind *is* man in the sense that interpretation of any of the existing bodies of knowledge leads back to the study of the human mind. "The encyclopedic order does not suppose that all the sciences are directly related to each other. They are branches that grow from a single trunk, knowledge of the human understanding. These branches often do not have any immediate connection between them, and many are only united by the trunk itself." [24]

Following the "metaphysical" exposition of the order and generation of the sciences comes D'Alembert's "historical" account of their progress since the rebirth of learning, an account in which the names of Bacon, Descartes, Newton, and Locke figure most prominently. D'Alembert distinguished this account from the one he had already given:

When one considers the progress of the mind since this memorable epoch, . . . one finds that this progress was made in the order that it was bound to follow. It began with erudition, continued through belles-lettres, and finished with philosophy. This order differs, indeed, from that which man must follow when abandoned to his own lights, or when limited to intercourse with his contemporaries, which is the order we have principally considered in the first part of this discourse; in fact, we have shown that

23. *Ibid.*, p. 234.   24. *Ibid.*, pp. 245–46.

the isolated spirit ought to encounter philosophy on its route before belles-lettres. But in emerging from the long period of ignorance that preceded the centuries of enlightenment, the regeneration of ideas . . . necessarily had to be different from their primitive generation.[25]

The order in which the sciences have developed historically is thus a lapse from the ideal (or, here, "primitive") order of the generation of ideas. If we attempt to relate these two orders as the stages of a temporal process, the progress of the human mind separates into three stages: (1) The original development of ideas out of sensations, in accordance with the metaphysical order of generation; (2) the intrusion of "history" with the coming of the Dark Ages; (3) the revival of interest in the classics, the first impetus given to free inquiry by Descartes and Bacon, Newton's triumph in the natural sciences, Locke's defining the proper vocation for philosophy, and his sketch of "the experimental physics of the soul." Beginning especially with Locke, there is the progressive discovery of the true order in the generation of ideas. This knowledge will help to wipe out the superstitions that are due to historical accident. If we accept the principle (as, for example, Chastellux argued) that man's fall from the metaphysical order is a consequence of his perfectibility, the problem in such a series is then to relate stages (2) and (3). How have men liberated themselves from their past? Do they also inherit Reason? And if Reason has always been present but has simply been hidden by the veil of custom, how has it happened that the veil has been torn away at the particular moment in history when it has? D'Alembert leaves these problems unanswered. He offers no explanation consistent with his general metaphysical principles which will also account specifically for the revolutionary revival of the sciences at the particular place and time at which the event took place. The old Cartesian separation of reason from historic change thus remains in this account of progress.

This problem of temporally relating the metaphysical order to the historic order was not, however, in the foreground of D'Alembert's mind. He was mainly interested in the development by philosophy of a critical instrument for the analysis and organization of science. Like his contemporaries, he obscured this interest by giving an account of the mind in the seemingly temporal terms of the order of the generation of ideas. But his interest here was not in history, but in philosophy.

25. *Ibid.,* p. 248.

It really made very little difference whether there had actually ever been an "isolated spirit" which followed the metaphysical order. Nor did D'Alembert expect human thinking to follow the metaphysical order once that order had been discovered. Rather, the metaphysical order would serve as an ideal in the light of which the failures of historic inquiry might be pointed out. Rousseau's warning at the beginning of his *Discourse on the Origin of Inequality* is characteristic of the Enlightenment attitude: "Let us begin then by laying facts aside as they do not affect the question. The investigations we may enter into, in treating this subject, must not be considered as historical truths, but only as mere conditional and hypothetical reasonings, rather calculated to explain the nature of things, than to ascertain their actual origin." [26]

The opening passages of the *Preliminary Discourse* bear evidence of this. The *use of* the "metaphysical order" was to show the specific and proper functions of the various sciences, and the reasons for their mistakes. The difficulty in D'Alembert's argument was not primarily that he constructed an imaginary history. Rather, it was that he urged that there were invariable principles of development, but also admitted at the same time that these principles did not actually function in the historic progress of the sciences. In the last analysis, this was the difficulty that was central to the metaphysical approach of the empiricists. It was illustrated in Condillac, with his two accounts of the development of knowledge, and in Turgot and Condorcet, among others. Their ideology did not consist so much in a confusion of metaphysics with history, but in the fact that they interpreted the actual history of knowledge in terms of an antecedent conception of the order and generation of ideas. The effect was to make the history of progress appear to be a lapse from a more proper and perfect order, an unhappy but necessary expedient.

D'ALEMBERT'S CULTURAL ACCOUNT OF SCIENCE

When he took up the history of the sciences, however, D'Alembert did not really employ this metaphysical standard. The notion of the historic continuity and the cumulative growth of the sciences figured

26. Rousseau, *The Social Contract and Discourses*, pp. 175–76.

much more largely as an instrument for explaining and judging their progress. While he held that the metaphysical order described the itinerary of "the isolated spirit," he explained the ages of ignorance by referring to the social environment: "The ideas that are acquired by reading and society are the germs of almost every discovery. It is an air that one breathes without thinking, and to which one owes his life; and the men of whom we speak were deprived of such help." [27] Again, D'Alembert criticized the tendency of many of his age to condemn outright the Renaissance interest in mere erudition. A century such as his, "which believes itself destined to change the laws in every field," should not dispense with what was usable in the past. Indeed, erudition might serve a philosophic, as well as merely an historical, interest: "In order to put us in a position to extract from the works of the ancients all that could be useful to us, it was necessary that they [the erudite] take from those works what was not." [28]

D'Alembert's account of the history of science was opposed to his inherited metaphysical predisposition to trace science back to its absolutely first beginning. The guiding principle in the latter part of the *Discourse* is that science has a general cultural setting, that it emerges out of a past, and this principle was also present in D'Alembert's consideration of the prospects of science. The latter part of the discourse attempts an appraisal of the intellectual wealth of the century. In this connection, D'Alembert's implicit assumption was that the progress of science was not only conditioned by the general state of a culture, but that it tended to be assimilated to that culture, and to reinforce the very conditions which were conducive to its growth. Such principles led D'Alembert to criticize the extremist tendencies of the attack upon the ancients.

Philosophy, which forms the dominant taste of our century, seems, through the progress it is making among us, to want to make up for lost time, and to avenge itself for the kind of stigma which our fathers had attached to it. Today, this stigma is fallen upon erudition. . . . It is imagined that we have taken from the works of the ancients all that it is important to know. . . . It is to be ignorant or presumptuous to believe . . . that we have nothing more of advantage to gain from the study and the reading of the ancients. [29]

27. D'Alembert, *Œuvres*, I, 249.
28. *Ibid.*, pp. 252–53.   29. *Ibid.*, pp. 284–85.

In the light of this interest in the broader cultural setting of science, D'Alembert's views concerning the past were not the simple ones of the Cartesian Malebranche. The introduction of the experimental method into physics and philosophy had made his age "modern" in the specific sense that it had reinforced the inclination, and provided the tools, for criticizing inherited materials. But it did not provide an excuse for dispensing with the past. The intellectual revolution indeed required that the past be viewed through the prism of the new enlightenment. But, conscious as he was of the continuity of an intellectual enterprise like the *Encyclopædia* with both past and future, D'Alembert did not think that everything in the past would turn out to be unilluminated.

One other element appears in D'Alembert's survey of the progress of science. D'Alembert's acute awareness of the impact of science upon culture led him to certain animadversions against the regnant "analytic method" that have the quality of both Rousseau and Diderot. Rousseau was not alone in his anxiety at the caricature of society as a jack-in-the-box to be pulled by enlightened philosophers. D'Alembert expressed disagreement with Rousseau's attack upon the arts and sciences, arguing that their "abolition" would leave the vices with us, and "we would have ignorance in addition." [30] But he shared the fear that simplistic analysis "murders, to dissect." And, like Diderot, he suggested the need for enlarging the method of philosophy so as to take account of more than the mechanistic. He feared that the anatomizing of a culture through the spread of analysis would kill the culture by stripping it of its felt values. The line between Rousseau and the men who remained within the Encyclopedist circle was not the simple one between "reason" and "emotion."

The best things are abused. This philosophic spirit, so much in fashion today, which wants to see everything and to suppose nothing, has spread

30. *Ibid.,* p. 297. But see Rousseau's own statement in *Rousseau juge de Jean-Jacques:* "He has obstinately been accused of wanting to destroy the sciences, arts, theatres, and academies, and to plunge the universe into its original barbarism; and he has insisted, on the contrary, upon conserving existing institutions, maintaining that their destruction could only remove the palliatives while leaving the vices." (Bayet and Albert, *Les écrivains politiques du 18e siècle,* pp. 243–44.)

into belles-lettres. . . . Our century, inclined as it is towards combination and analysis, seems to want to introduce cold and didactic discussions into the things of sentiment. It is not that the passions and taste do not have their own logic: but this logic has principles entirely different from those of the ordinary logic. . . . It has to be acknowledged that this spirit of discussion has helped to free our literature from blind admiration of the ancients. . . . But this anatomy of the soul has insinuated itself into our conversations; they are dissertations, not conversations; and our society has lost its outstanding charms, warmth and gaiety.[31]

TURGOT: PROGRESS AND PROVIDENCE

The idea that science operated within a cultural context, and that it was a factor in freeing other institutions from prejudice, encrusted tradition, and ignorance, became a guiding principle for the understanding of history in the work of Voltaire and D'Alembert. Their histories gave impetus to the belief in social progress. Society would improve insofar as it was permeated by the methods and results of science. Since "science" sometimes meant one thing, however, and sometimes another, the idea of social progress had varying connotations. The growth of science in comprehensiveness and reliability might be explained in terms of its method as, for example, in Pascal and Fontenelle, or it might be explained in terms of larger metaphysical conceptions. If the latter were used, the continuous and cumulative growth of human reason became a condition for the growth of science rather than a consequence of its establishment. This made a very great difference. Men and nations would grow wiser as they grew older even if they possessed no method for learning from experience. The belief in progress could be held as a necessary inference from the laws of nature.

The figure of Turgot is perhaps outstanding in this respect. Turgot's belief in the ubiquity of law, making for the continuous growth of reason through history, was indeed so strong that he seems somewhat separate from the rest of the *philosophes*. The principle of the ubiquity of reason imparted to Turgot's speculations on progress a much greater emphasis on the reasonableness of what had happened,

31. D'Alembert, *Œuvres*, I, 289-91.

and much less emphasis upon the curious lapses from reason that, for example, strew the pages of Voltaire's histories. Like Voltaire and the *philosophes,* Turgot found "sects" pernicious, but he was apparently more sensitive than others to the fact that the Encyclopedists themselves might be, or become, a sect, and he consequently laid great stress on the processes of cross-fertilization that enriched seemingly opposed doctrines. In July of 1750, Turgot delivered a discourse at the Sorbonne, *On the Advantages that the Establishment of Christianity Has Brought for the Human Race.* His argument was that Christianity had been one of the most important factors that had made for progress. It had saved antiquity from superstition, had preserved the sciences through ages that would otherwise have been completely dark, and had presented to the minds of men the emancipating conception of a law transcending individual human interests and prejudices.

In order to bring back rights and justice a principle was necessary which could lift men out of themselves and of all that surrounds them, which could make them envisage every nation and every condition with an equitable view. . . . That is what religion has done. . . . Could one hope for this from any other principle than religion? What else could have been able to combat and vanquish the alliance of interest and prejudice? The Christian religion alone has succeeded. It alone has brought to light the rights of humanity. . . .[32]

   Turgot's theory of progress placed emphasis upon the continuity between past and present, rather than upon purging the present of the vestiges of its unenlightened ancestry. His fundamental principle was that human communication is the basis of progress, that language is the essential medium for the preservation and transmission of the historically accumulated intellectual wealth to which every generation makes its own contribution. It is, consequently, the arts of communication like writing and printing which are of critical importance.

All the ages are linked by a series of causes and effects which bind the present situation of the world to all those that have preceded. The multifarious signs of language and writing, in giving men the means of assuring themselves of the possession of their ideas, and of communicating them to others, have turned every individual discovery into a common treasure, which one generation transmits to another, so as to grant a constantly aug-

32. Turgot, *Œuvres,* II, 43, 47–48.

mented heritage to each century; and the human species considered from its origin appears to the eyes of a philosopher as an immense whole, which has, like every individual, its childhood and its progress.[33]

Turgot found continuity everywhere, and wherever he found continuity he inferred progress. More clearly than anyone else among the *philosophes* who came before Condorcet, Turgot formulated the conception of necessary and inevitable progress. Universal history was ultimately a study in the progress of mankind. Turgot's conception approached the philosophy of history of St. Augustine or Bossuet in finding every historic event to be meaningful as part of the unitary, all-embracing movement of the human race towards its goal. There were not several human histories, nor several lines of continuity, nor various possible outcomes; there was only one history with one meaning and outcome possible for it.

Universal history embraces the consideration of the successive stages in the progress of the human species, and the specific causes that have contributed to it; the formation and mixing of nations; the origins, the revolutions of governments; the progress of languages, of physics, of morals, of manners, of the sciences and arts; the revolutions which have made Empires succeed Empires, nations follow on nations, religions on religions; the human species, always the same through these upheavals, and constantly advancing towards its perfection.[34]

There was thus a kind of cosmic Toryism about Turgot's philosophy of progress. Nothing in history was wasted, nothing did not turn out in the end to have promoted human happiness. Every event was continuous with every other, and progress followed automatically from the communication of ideas. Every human experience became part of the historic tradition with which men work, and was therefore automatically instructive. "No mutation has taken place which has not brought some advantage; because none has been made without producing some experience, and without extending or improving or preparing instruction." [35] Indeed, not only truth and reason, but error and passion as well, have been factors in progress. "The real advancement of the human mind is revealed even in its aberrations." [36]

33. *Ibid.*, pp. 52–53. See pp. 59–60 as well, for Turgot's discussion of writing and printing.
34. *Ibid.*, p. 212.   35. *Ibid.*, p. 229.   36. *Ibid.*, p. 90.

Turgot went farther than the position that error had in fact turned out to be the precursor and sufficient condition for the discovery of truth. For Turgot, who applied the idea of the necessary Order of Nature to history and time, it was an essential condition as well. Not only did everything have a place in nature but no two things could exchange places, and this was true for the dimension of time as well as for space. This temporalizing of the conception of the harmonious and economical Order of Nature resulted in Turgot's theory of progress, and led, for example, to the conclusion that at certain stages in history reason would have been an obstacle to progress because it would have retarded communication. "The passions multiplied ideas, extended knowledge, perfected minds in the absence of reason, whose day had not yet come, and which would have been less powerful if it had reigned earlier. . . . Reason and justice, better understood, would have fixed everything, as has nearly happened in China." [37]

Turgot developed this conception that progress moves through necessary stages into two laws of social development. The first was a principle of historic acceleration: every progressive step causes an acceleration in the rate of progress; and since every historic event was progressive in function, the principle implies that the tempo of historic change necessarily increases steadily. The second was that intellectual development must go through three necessary stages: (1) the explanation of events in terms of spiritual powers; (2) the explanation of events in terms of essences and powers; (3) the mechanistic explanation of events. No stage can be eliminated, nor can the necessary order of succession be changed. Turgot stated these laws only in passing, but they have had a significant influence. In the next century Auguste Comte took up Turgot's observation and developed systematically the positivist conception of the three stages of progress—the theological, the metaphysical, and the positive.

Turgot was aware of the gap that existed between his *a priori* affirmation of progress and the evidence found when the actual record of human history was appraised. "But what a spectacle is presented by the succession of the opinions of men! I seek there for the progress of the human mind, and I see almost nothing but the history of its errors." [38] His attempt to resolve the paradox was ingenious. Turgot

37. *Ibid.*, pp. 225–26.   38. *Ibid.*, p. 60.

fell back upon Condillac's empiricist account of the development of
ideas. We have seen that in Condillac's theory the progress of empirical knowledge rested upon chance, that is, upon the uncontrolled
presentation of new sensations. Turgot employed this notion to explain the origin (and necessity) of error. The slower advance of the
empirical sciences as compared with mathematics was due to the fact
that the empirical sciences depended upon chance experience. The
conceptions contained in the empirical sciences "are not collections of
ideas that the mind forms of its own accord, and whose extent it
knows precisely. The ideas are born and combine in our soul almost
without our knowing. . . ." [39]

Turgot's appeal to chance is illustrative of the disproportionately
large part that accident or chance tend to play in a philosophy of history that holds all events to have but one meaning. All events in general are explained in terms of the *a priori* assumptions of continuity
and necessity—that everything that is partakes of what has been, and
that what is could not have come about in any other way. But when the
specific question is asked, "Why this particular error at this particular
time?" Turgot must appeal to chance. That we sometimes "learn by
trial and error" in the sense that certain errors have preceded truthful
discoveries is one thing; but it is a very different thing to assert that
those particular errors had to be made in order to discover the truth,
or that all errors ultimately issue in discovery. In *general,* Turgot argued, it is "reason" that makes this take place; but, in any *particular*
case, it is chance. He gave no details of the manner in which errors
were converted into truths, asserting that we learn continuously from
error apart from any specific method for learning from experience.
Turgot's ingenuity lay in his attempt to exploit the Cartesian separation of history from philosophy for the purpose of explaining the
ubiquity of error in a world that was entirely progressive. But his
generalization that all errors were instructive removed him from the
more experimental tradition of Pascal, who emphasized the specific
method of experimental science as the condition for the cumulative
efficiency of inquiry. In experimental science larger, more general systems are developed from the smaller systems that have already been
incorporated into the structure of science. In this process these smaller

39. *Ibid.,* pp. 60–61.

systems are corrected as they are enlarged, and consequently, if one wishes to stretch the term, one may, looking at them retrospectively, call them "errors," and speak of the progress of truth "over the ruins of 'false' opinions." But to speak of the usefulness of smaller systems, which have been incorporated into the structure of science, in the pursuit of truth is very different from speaking of the general "necessity" of errors that have not been part of the history of organized experimental inquiry. Was the opinion, for example, that the earth was flat a necessary prerequisite to the discovery that it is round?

Turgot's philosophy restated Fontenelle's observation that the history of science was marked by the progress of truth over the ruins of inadequate opinions. But Turgot went on to convert this empirical observation into a universal and necessary principle, affirming that every error was necessary for truth. In the last analysis, his philosophy of history contained the difficulties of any monistic theory which sees all events necessarily converging upon a single goal. There is a teleology in his theory, no less real because it is suppressed than the teleology of St. Augustine. The lines of continuity which we explore when we move back in time carry us out in many directions; to urge, as did Turgot, that they all necessarily converge suggests not only that they were all evaluated from one point of view, but that Turgot had an antecedent certainty that history has a single goal. Further, under what conditions might we test Turgot's hypothesis? An empirical test of the proposition that all events are progressive must permit of the possibility of a negative instance. But it is precisely the point of Turgot's theory to rule out such a possibility. Everything may be interpreted as progressive in the light of his *a priori* assurance concerning communication and continuity.

A monistic philosophy of history, as Turgot's illustrates, makes it difficult to make moral distinctions, and implicitly disparages the creative role of human will or intelligence in history. In the last analysis, Turgot had only two alternatives. On the basis of his monistic assumption that all human experience was continuous and cumulative, he could assert that we *must* learn from error, that progress was necessary: but the consequence of this alternative would be to make it impossible to apply a standard of progress to any specific case, because, since everything is defined *a priori* as progressive, it is impossible to distinguish between particular progressive and non-progressive events. The second alternative was simply to depend on chance. For if progress depended on no specific condition such as the presence of a peculiar method, what guaranteed its continuation? What, apart from a *fortuitous chance,* or a providential concurrence of events, could guarantee that we should continue to learn from our errors?

THE SECULARIZATION OF PROVIDENCE

Universal history was thus a grand unit, a course of events that took on significance in the light of a single, all-embracing goal towards which it moved inexorably. The coming together of Progress and Providence in the work of Turgot is so striking that one might hold him to be a rebel against the dominant empiricism, the growing naturalism, and the struggling secularism of his age. It would be wrong to imagine, however, that Turgot did not share the *philosophes'* excitement at the development of science, or that, because he held that Christianity was a "progressive force," he did not share the worldly values of his contemporaries. Turgot's philosophy marks a stage in the secularization of the idea of Providence. He held Christianity to be progressive because it had promoted and preserved science, and because it was an indispensable agent in the making of good citizens. Turgot's measures of progress, as they emerge at the end of his *Second Discourse,* are the degree to which the sciences are progressively unified, the extent to which they mark the quality of public enlightenment, and the degree to which their methods are made more efficient. These are Encyclopedic ideals.

Furthermore, Turgot attributed to the analytic method the same power as did his contemporaries—the power of undermining authority and its intellectual ally, the *esprit de système;* and his specific evaluations of particular historical events (such as despotism) were anything but the complacent reactions of a cosmic Tory. Turgot's view took on a critical, rather than apologetic, direction in his sporadic emphasis on the crucial significance of analysis as a continuous and critical refinement of grosser modes of communication. It was this idea of analysis as a working factor within and upon a culture that was seized upon by Condorcet. What obscured its significance in Turgot's philosophy was his disposition to hold that progress would take place in any case—a position that made the specific function of a cumulative and critical method seem relatively unimportant.

VII

Custom and Nature

> But what is nature? Why is custom
> not natural? I much fear that this
> nature is itself only a first custom, as
> custom is second nature. (Pascal)

CONDORCET'S TWO INTERPRETATIONS OF SCIENCE

No BOOK so well reveals the climate of opinion of the French Enlightenment as Condorcet's *Progress of the Human Mind*. The book registered the conviction of the Age of Reason that the liberation of intelligence through organized science, and the spread of the authority and temper of mind represented by science, was the age's great achievement, and its unique contribution to the future. More single-mindedly than anyone else, Condorcet presented the progress of the human mind as the history of the impact of the scientific discipline upon religious, political, and social relationships. His essay was the attempt to illuminate the conditions and the meaning of the growth of science, and to lay down the program for those who were its trustees.

Everything tells us that we are approaching the era of one of the grand revolutions of the human race. What can better enlighten us as to what we may expect, what can be a surer guide to us, amidst its commotions, than the picture of the revolutions that have preceded and prepared the way for it? The present state of knowledge assures us that it will be happy. But is it not upon condition that we know how to assist it with all our strength?[1]

Condorcet's book was only a preliminary draft, in which he set down in some haste the various questions that, in his view, ought to

1. Condorcet, *The Progress of the Human Mind*, p. 19.

be discussed in a systematic treatment of the progress of the human mind. It is divided into ten "epochs," and prefaced by an introductory section. Each *Epoch* is distinguished in terms of the distinctive problems that confronted it, and its story told in terms of the solutions of these problems, solutions which constituted its historic contribution. Condorcet wrote at random, and the points of continuity between the epochs were often vague or only implied. Nevertheless, his conviction that the revolutionary growth of enlightenment was the distinctive feature of his day provided a unifying principle of selection and evaluation. The rise and fall of nations, war and peace, the growth of commerce and communication, the expansion of Europe, were all considered in terms of their contribution to the progress of enlightenment.

Both of the inconsistent interpretations of the intellectual revolution represented by science which we have been examining reached full development in Condorcet's book and governed his reflections. In the first place, Condorcet accepted the "metaphysical" empiricist account of the development of the mind, and he retained the Cartesian ideal of a science of infallible truths. This gave to his theory the paradoxical character of the theories of Chastellux and Volney. Stressing, on the one hand, the continuous growth of reason, he also stressed, on the other, the revolutionary struggle and victory of reason against the dark ages of crime and folly. When he interpreted it in the Cartesian manner as a revelation of ultimate truths, Condorcet might have made the same remark with respect to the new science which Tertullian had made about the Christian revelation—that the simplest mechanic of his day was superior to the philosopher of previous times because he could answer questions that lay beyond the powers of any mind unillumined by the new and special Revelation. The progress of science in the discovery of such truths as natural rights and the empiricist simple sensations was of revolutionary significance, and had placed the human mind and human society for the first time on a valid foundation.

Condorcet's second interpretation of the meaning of the new science, however, did not rest so much upon the metaphysical hypostatization of science as upon the *method* of science. Condorcet sometimes thought of science not as a body of perfect truths but as an integrated way of making and holding judgments. This second interpretation was rarely explicitly separated from the first, nor did Condorcet seem to sense any inconsistency in using both interpretations. But at critical moments in his argument—especially in the *Tenth Epoch*—he sometimes used this second interpretation systematically and exclusively. The method of science was such that the scientific tradition was distinguished from other traditions. Science grew continuously and cumulatively, and corrected itself as it developed. Given the *method* of science, one might predict that, other things being equal, knowledge would grow steadily more comprehensive and reliable. Scientific method, in short, offered a model of actual progress.

There were of course clear-cut precedents in Pascal and Fontenelle for this observation. But Condorcet added to it the awareness, which had been so greatly stimulated by Voltaire, of the cultural conditions and implications of the scientific temper of mind. Neither technologically nor culturally could a community remain the same once science had intruded upon it. Science provided powers over physical nature, but its restless, questioning, positivistic spirit also affected human behavior by a kind of contagion, and brought new values and new standards to the fore. Nor was science limited merely to destroying inherited moralities. The scientific community, "the phalanx of philosophic spirits," presented a model of a new and improved morality.

The notion that Condorcet believed that men could be brought to act in mechanical conformity with a prearranged plan is at best a half-truth. He was anything but blind to the influence on human conduct of habit, sectarian interest, and the passions, and he was only too aware that non-intellectual factors had played, and were continuing to play, roles in human history. Although his metaphysical faith in human perfectibility played a part, it was not that alone which brought him to prophesy the triumph of human reason over prejudice and absolutism. There was also before him the *fact* of enlightenment, a custom that was becoming, as it were, "second nature," offering an alternative way of behavior to that dominated by clerical pretension or uncontrolled caprice. Sensitive to the changes science had wrought on the European scene, Condorcet saw the new era in possession of a distinctive opportunity: science presented a new *method* of social change that might be substituted for methods issuing from ignorance and eventuating in violence.

Several strands thus come together in Condorcet's book: the "metaphysics" of the "isolated spirit," and of science as a body of finished conclusions; the contrasting emphasis of Pascal and Fontenelle upon the *method* of science as the condition of *controlled* progress, rather than automatic progress or chance progress; and the cultural emphasis of Voltaire and D'Alembert. When Condorcet approached the cultural context and significance of science from the point of view of the "isolated spirit," he saw it as the historic opposition of the forces of truth and the forces of superstition; when, on the other hand, he approached it from the point of view of *method,* he saw the significance of science to reside in the loosening of the cake of custom in every field by the critical habits, the organized modernity, of scientific practice. Further, he saw the method of science as the model of a new morality, suggesting new social values and altering the traditional conception of the content of happiness. Thus, when Condorcet spoke of progress he meant any one of three things—(1) the simple linear accumulation of ideas with more experience; (2) the continuing successful struggle for the emancipation of reason from its enemies, "in which . . . it throws off, one by one, the remainder of its fetters"; [2] and (3) the increasing facility, efficiency, and control of inherited ideas that comes with the systematic practice of scientific method.

METAPHYSICS AND HISTORY

Condorcet's book begins with the empiricist account of the mind. This is "metaphysics," Condorcet tells us, when "we confine our observations to an enquiry into the general facts and unvarying laws which the development of these faculties presents to us, in what is common to the different individuals of the human species." The development of ideas is "historical," however, when we consider it "in its results, relative to the mass of individuals co-existing at the same time on a given space, and follow it from generation to generation,"

2. *Ibid.,* p. 225.

and when the picture of human progress is formed "by the successive observation of human societies at the different eras through which they have passed." The difference between the metaphysical and historical picture of the progress of the human mind is presumably that the latter deals with a great number of individuals united in society. "This progress," writes Condorcet, "is subject to the same general laws, observable in the individual development of our faculties; being the result of that very development considered at once in a great number of individuals united in society." [3]

One may suspect, however, that a deeper distinction is involved. Metaphysics is concerned with "general facts and unvarying laws," while history is concerned with individual events taking place at specific, unrepeatable times. Condorcet seems to have been aware that the element of contingency played a greater part in history than in metaphysics. For example, after asserting the applicability of metaphysical law to history, he adds immediately, *"But* the result which every instant presents depends upon that of the preceding instants, and has an influence on the instants which follow. This picture, therefore, is historical . . . subjected as it will be to *perpetual variations."* [4]

The relation between "metaphysics" and "history" in Condorcet is both vague and complex. The attempt to give historical explanations that openly involve an appeal to unvarying laws is probably preferable to the covert use of unanalyzed theories of human nature which we find in many less openly "rationalistic" histories. Furthermore, the notion of an ideal order of invariant relationships which is applicable, "other things being equal," to human affairs has, whatever its weaknesses, certain obvious advantages over the mere accumulation of great masses of unrelated "empirical" information unillumined by an explicitly stated conceptual system. But Condorcet used metaphysical laws to construct speculative history when there were no available records.[5] And he also admitted, like D'Alembert, that much of recorded history was contrary to the "natural" and "normal" succession of things as presented by metaphysics. Indeed, even if we should believe that Condorcet's metaphysical psychology actually describes what would happen were there no "social" influences, the hypostatiza-

3. *Ibid.,* pp. 2–3.   4. *Ibid.,* p. 3. Italics mine.
5. See, for example, the *First Epoch.*

tion of this order as "natural" and "normal" is dangerous since it diverts attention from explaining those events that do not fit the ideal pattern. These become impediments in the system, and impediments become inherently contingent events for which no logical order can be found. For there is ultimately only one order, both natural and ideal, and everything else is simply dis-order. Instead of progressively eliminating the unsystematized area in historical knowledge, Condorcet's metaphysics thus served to divert attention from the study of the specific factors in a given historical situation. What could not be explained by appeal to the unvarying laws was merely an accident, and the key question of fitting the accident into a system (so that it was no longer a complete accident) was neglected. The Cartesian dualism thus persisted.

Insofar as Condorcet leaned on his metaphysics, his argument developed similarly to Turgot's. In the natural order of things progress was inexorable and error had its proper place. The fact of progress followed from the general laws of the development of human faculties. Condorcet's actual practice, however, ran beyond the confines of his theory. To be sure, he often interpreted specific events as "accidents" and attempted no explanation of them. On the other hand, he only rarely invoked directly the general laws of the development of the "isolated spirit" in explaining "the influence of every past period upon that which follows it." His historical (as opposed to his metaphysical) approach led him to consider the capacities of individuals as functions of a culturally accumulated fund of techniques, and carried him beyond the individualistic metaphysical psychology with which he began in keeping with the convention of his day. There can be little doubt that Condorcet took this convention seriously. Nevertheless, a good deal of what followed his initial statement of principle had little logical connection with it.

THE STRUGGLE BETWEEN TRUTH AND ERROR

While Condorcet began by affirming that the present was the child of the past and the parent of the future, the body of his work was anything but an illustration of the principle of historic continuity.

Much as he admired Turgot, he was more of a sectarian and a missionary,[6] and the history of human progress as it unfolds in his book is the story of the relentless struggle between truth and error, nature and custom, liberty and authority.

Condorcet's survey of the past was governed largely by his hatred of the priests. He regarded religion as priestcraft and the priests as mainly responsible for retarding the progress of reason. The clergy had monopolized enlightenment and maintained it as a monastic mystery long after the need for their isolated, hot-house cultivation of learning had disappeared. In the age-old struggle for progress, the black days were those of the ascendancy of religion. Christianity had been a persistent barrier to the advance of humanity.

Contempt of human sciences was one of the first features of Christianity. It had to avenge itself for the outrages of philosophy; it feared that spirit of investigation and doubt, that confidence of man in his own reason, the pest alike of all religious creeds. . . . The triumph of Christianity was thus the signal for the entire decline both of the sciences and of philosophy.[7]

The figures whom Condorcet singled out as the heroes of the struggle of reason against organized superstition suggest the main phases of the battle. In the war against the repressive clerical cartel, the first signal victories had been won by Bacon, Galileo, and Descartes. Descartes especially had brought to mankind, if not liberation from its inherited corruption, at least the opportunity to be saved.

The transition from the epoch we have been considering to that which follows, has been distinguished by three extraordinary personages, Bacon, Galileo, and Descartes. . . .

6. In his *Vie de Turgot* Condorcet tried to explain and mitigate Turgot's defense of Christianity. "M. Turgot did not hide from himself either the frightful abuses of ecclesiastical power, . . . or the bloody quarrels of *sacerdotium* and *imperium,* or the baneful maxims of the clergy. . . . The blood of several million men, massacred in the name of God, still reeking about us. . . . Could a pure and noble soul not be aroused? . . . M. Turgot . . . was aware that if everyone . . . whose opinion really governs the world should cease to be united in a spirit of tolerance and reason, then the same causes would soon produce the same effects. But M. Turgot believed this revolution to be impossible. . . ." (*Œuvres,* V, 10–13.)

7. Condorcet, *The Progress of the Human Mind,* p. 128.

Endowed with a master genius for the sciences, Descartes joined example to precept, in exhibiting the method of finding and ascertaining truth.

He wished to extend his method to every object of human intelligence; God, man, the universe, were in turn the subject of his meditations. . . . The very boldness of his errors was instrumental to the progress of the human species. He gave activity to minds which the circumspection of his rivals could not awake from their lethargy. He called upon men to throw off the yoke of authority, to acknowledge no influence but what reason should avow: and he was obeyed, because he subjected by his daring, and fascinated by his enthusiasm.[8]

Descartes had been the instigator of modernity as an organized force. He had stimulated a habit of mind, a restlessness, a pervasive appeal to reason, which knew no bounds. He had been the prophet of the triumph of reason.

Following Descartes, Newton had given the climactic proof of the powers of reason, demonstrating that the new method led to organized and complete knowledge of the physical world. And with Newton's triumph a new class of men emerged upon the European scene— Condorcet's own ancestors, the first professional intellectuals, the precursors of the *esprit philosophique,* who turned a series of unrelated skirmishes into what was almost an organized campaign. The man of letters had come forward to perform liaison duties, spreading a habit of mind which had first taken root among intellectuals, and extending the scope and changing the quality of the problems and interests to which this habit was considered germane. It was they who made plain the practical meaning of Descartes' appeal to the indubitable fact of his own mind. Men learned that they might subject every opinion to the test of reason, that their own minds were indeed their only means for the discovery of truth, and that they were not condemned to resting uncritically upon the judgments of others. The men of letters fought the battle for freedom of thought: their object was not so much to discover new truths as to represent and disseminate the new spirit, and it was they who had rallied men with the cry of *reason, toleration,* and *humanity.*

Locke had won the decisive battle. To be sure, an intimation of his principles might be found in Aristotle, to whom "we owe that important truth, that first step in the science of the human mind, that

8. *Ibid.,* pp. 220–23.

our ideas, even such as are most abstract, most strictly intellectual, so to speak, *have their origin in our sensations.*" [9] But in Aristotle this had been merely an intuition rather than a systematically developed philosophy. Locke had provided the method for analyzing ideas empirically, which guaranteed that reason would never again degenerate. For now true ideas could be obtained purposively, and morality would rest on necessary and immutable laws. "In a word, the progress of the human mind in every species of enquiry was regulated by this principle." [10] On the basis of Locke's principles, and confronted by the new power to control human affairs which Locke had provided, Turgot, Price, and Priestley had elaborated the idea of the indefinite progress of the human mind. The stage was thus set for the "tenth epoch," a future of assured progress.

THE SOCIOLOGY OF ERROR

Condorcet's account of the historic struggle between truth and error contained the suggestions of two general principles which have been of considerable importance in later historical and sociological investigation. The first was a principle of cultural lag. Condorcet argued that errors arise in the natural course of inquiry. As inquiry progresses truths are discovered that replace these errors. Nevertheless, the errors persist. "Men retain the errors of their infancy, their country, and the age in which they live, long after the truths necessary to the removal of these errors are acknowledged." [11] Reason has to struggle constantly against lagging habits and customs.

Had Condorcet confined his explanation to this principle of historic inertia he might be accused of having fallen into the genetic fallacy of believing that the mere discovery of the origin of a belief or institution "explained" it. But Condorcet was not completely unaware of the further question, "Why do given errors persist?" Why do some habits of behavior show greater staying power than others? To argue simply that the present was continuous with the past, or that "habit" in general was the cause of cultural lag, was not enough. It was in response to this problem that Condorcet's second generalization took

9. *Ibid.,* p. 107.   10. See *ibid.,* pp. 240–43.   11. *Ibid.,* p. 16.

shape. It concerned the phases in the history of a social class—its emergence as a "progressive force" serving the underlying purpose of history, its gradual perversion of its original historic purpose to its own interest, and its ultimate decrepitude and degeneration. The principle was more implicit than explicit, underlying his treatment of the relationship of the clergy to enlightenment, and reflecting his antecedent convictions concerning the underlying purpose and direction of history: for a "progressive force" is one that is in the main stream of history, which is another way of saying that it is one which serves the interests that the particular historian finds important. For it is in the light of these interests that he distinguishes the main stream from the minor eddies, the relevant from the irrelevant, and the continuous from the discontinuous.

Nevertheless, Condorcet's principle was suggestive. It had distinct merits as compared to a general appeal to habit alone, or to a completely individualistic psychology. It focussed attention on discernible human purposes, and it introduced a distinctively sociological approach by calling attention to the changed functioning of human purposes when they become the institutionalized purposes of social groups. Indeed, not only was this principle not to be inferred from Condorcet's *a priori* acceptance of the individualistic metaphysics of the isolated spirit, but it cast considerable suspicion on the *a priori* belief in the harmony of nature.

Condorcet explained cultural lag as due to more than mere habit. It was an effect of the existence within society of specialized classes with vested interests in maintaining outmoded conventions. The prejudices of philosophers sometimes prevent the discovery of new truths; popular prejudices impede their propagation; and esteemed and powerful professions struggle against enlightenment. "These are the three kinds of enemies which reason is continually obliged to encounter, and over which she frequently does not triumph till after a long and painful struggle." [12] Especially is the last of these a formidable and continuing enemy of progress. Esteemed and powerful professions devoted to learning arise in the very first "epoch" of human progress, and, so general and constant is such a development among all societies, that Condorcet believes it "to have a foundation in nature itself . . . in the

12. *Ibid.,* p. 17.

state of the human faculties at this early period of society." [13] When these classes first arise the essential harmony of human interest with the natural order is once more displayed. For the emergence of such a class had served a beneficent purpose. It had once been, in the not dissimilar words of contemporary Marxists, a "progressive force." The emergence of a class distinctively devoted to learning "enriched the sciences with new truths." And such a class had been necessary. "The sciences would have remained for a longer period in a state of earliest infancy, if certain families, and especially particular castes, had not made them the first foundation of their reputation and power." [14]

At this point, however, the harmony of human interest with nature appears to break down. For if a learned caste had come at the "necessary" time to serve its function it ought also to have left the stage of history once it was no longer "necessary." But this it did not do. Instead, it developed a kind of institutional momentum, an interest simply in maintaining itself; and to this end it employed its special knowledge. This learned class, of which "we still see the remains in our priests," took on the changed function of propagating error.

We can here perceive the beginnings of an institution, that in its progress has been attended with opposite effects, accelerating the advancement of knowledge, at the same time that it disseminated error. . . .

I mean the formation of a class of men, the depositaries of the elements of the sciences or processes of the arts, of the mysteries or ceremonies of religion, of the practices of superstition, and frequently even of the secrets of legislation and polity. I mean that separation of the human race into two portions; the one destined to teach, the other to believe; the one proudly concealing what it vainly boasts of knowing, the other receiving with respect whatever its teachers shall condescend to reveal; the one wishing to raise itself above reason, the other humbly renouncing reason, and debasing itself below humanity, by acknowledging in its fellow men prerogatives superior to their common nature.[15]

In time the class of learned men develops new tools, but the stratification remains.

Already the observation of man and of societies had been connected with that of nature. Already a small number of moral maxims, of a practical, as well as a political kind, had been transmitted from generation to genera-

13. *Ibid.*, pp. 27–28.   14. *Ibid.*, p. 57.   15. *Ibid.*, pp. 27–28.

tion. These were seized upon by those castes: religious ideas, prejudices, and different superstitions contributed to a still farther increase of their power. They succeeded the first associations, of first families, of empirics and sorcerers; but they practised more art to deceive and seduce the mind, which was now less rude and ignorant. . . . The members of these societies pursued at first, almost with equal ardour, two very different objects: one, that of acquiring for themselves new information; the other, that of employing such as they had already acquired in deceiving the people, and gaining an ascendancy over their minds. . . . These men had therefore two doctrines, one for themselves, the other for the people. Frequently even, as they were divided into many orders, each order reserved to itself its own mysteries. All the inferior orders were at once both knaves and dupes; and it was only by a few adepts that all the mazes of this hypocritical system were understood and developed.[16]

And finally the process becomes self-stultifying. The one-time progressive class, which had taken the special interest in science that had been required, had become stagnant and unproductive, and, in the end, ceased to preserve even what learning it had possessed.

Men, whose interest it was to deceive, soon felt a dislike to the pursuit of truth. Content with the docility of the people, they conceived there was no need of further means to secure its continuance. By degrees they forgot a part of the truths concealed under their allegories; they preserved no more of their ancient science than was strictly necessary to maintain the confidence of their disciples; and at last they became themselves the dupes of their own fables.

Then was all progress of the sciences at a stand; some even of those which had been enjoyed by preceding ages, were lost to the generations that followed; and the human mind, a prey to ignorance and prejudice, was condemned, in those vast empires, to a shameful stagnation. . . .[17]

This historical generalization, reminiscent in some respects of Rousseau's criticism of the division between knowledge and conscience, offered the basic reason why the history of the past was so largely a record of error, crime, and despotism. Mainly because it had been to the special interest of privileged classes, knowledge had been turned into a mystery of revelation, and had been employed as a weapon to keep power over the uninitiated populace. The contemporaneous tendency of European nations to exploit primitive peoples, and the habitual concurrence of the clergy in the despotic suppression of enlightened

16. *Ibid.*, pp. 57–58, 61–62.   17. *Ibid.*, pp. 66–67.

opinion, were for Condorcet current illustrations of this persistent tendency.

Condorcet's suggestive "sociology of error" raises, however, certain questions about his own "sociology of truth." Most of the *philosophes* believed that political progress should take place from the top down. Enlightened men would give the law to society in the interest not of themselves but of common (and unenlightened) humanity. Now why should the special class of intellectuals of the eighteenth century be expected to use their enlightenment for the good of suppressed classes? What in their character is different from that of other learned classes? Why not one more dictatorship of philosophers, or technicians, or managers? To be sure, Condorcet was more or less exceptional among the *philosophes* in his conviction that enlightenment should be extended beyond the *bon bourgeois*. But the problem is connected with a more fundamental issue. The sociological account of error makes it especially difficult to understand why men should be expected to make a new revelation of truth a controlling factor in their behavior. They will use it as a tool to serve class interests, but their class interests will not be affected by their knowledge.

It is this problem and similar ones which make Condorcet's second interpretation of science, in terms of its method, of such critical importance to his theory. As we shall see, had he consistently used such an interpretation, the problem of the relationship of the community of learned men to general social progress would have been substantially altered. For insofar as science was interpreted within the Cartesian categories, it became simply a set of intellectual affirmations with no effect on human inclination. There was nothing in the nature of science which would necessarily make an entrenched class give up its power, and very much in it that could be used by this class to entrench itself still further. There was no necessary relation between the intellectual recognition of natural rights and the obligation to take practical action. And there was, consequently, no indissoluble tie between the progress of knowledge, conceived in this manner, and the pursuit of happiness. Condorcet sometimes sounded like Rousseau, asking for a change of heart. The difference was that Condorcet seemed to take a change of heart as "reasonable," and that he looked upon it as a consequence of, rather than a prelude to, the progress of knowledge.

THE PARADOX OF PROGRESS

As we have noted, Condorcet's view of progress as a battle between opposing forces was the immediate result of practical efforts against clerical domination. The theoretical basis of his philosophy of history, with its dualistic Augustinian structure, lay in the pervasive Cartesian ideal of science. Condorcet held the Cartesian view that true science rested on infallible and necessary, that is, unquestionable and irrefutable, first principles. So interpreted, the new science seemed to rest on a kind of revelation and seemed to promise a revolution.

Condorcet's account of the mind purported to be one part of a general system of nature developed entirely in terms of the basic categories of Newtonian physics. In these terms, all errors in morals and philosophy necessarily went back to errors in physics.[18] One aspect of Condorcet's antecedent ideology was reflected in his attempt to explain the progress of human knowledge, not on the basis of observation of the actual practice of intellectual method, but on the basis of certain generalizations carried over by analogy from the field of physics—generalizations disengaged, on the one hand, from the specific procedures and subject-matter in which they functioned, and neglecting, on the other hand, the qualitative differences in subject-matter. His empiricist psychology provided him with a metaphysical guarantee for the analytic method, and, in consequence, Condorcet converted terms that had a meaning within a specific method and context into terms that had an absolute, unchanging meaning no matter what the context. Everything was ultimately composed of simples, nor could any combination of the ultimate simple elements display any property not originally contained in one or another of the separate elements. This was an instance of the mechanistic materialism Diderot was trying to avoid.

This ideology affected Condorcet's view of the science of man. He considered this science to be ideally a system of fixed principles deductively elaborated. The great antidote to the rule of passion and prejudice was the fixity of well-established truth. Thus, social progress

18. See *ibid.*, pp. 298–300.

among the Greeks, for example, had been practically non-existent because "politics had not yet acquired principles sufficiently invariable
not to fear that the legislators might introduce into these institutions
their prejudices and their passions." [19] Mankind's political liberation
had begun with the discovery of the true foundations of political
society. The habit of being moral would follow from correct calculation, just as vice was the result of false moral arithmetic.

It will be impossible for men to become enlightened upon the nature and
development of their moral sentiments, upon the principles of morality,
upon the motives for conforming their conduct to those principles, and
upon their interests, whether relative to their individual or social capacity,
without making, at the same time, an advancement in moral practice, not
less real than that of the science itself. Is not a mistaken interest the most
frequent cause of actions contrary to the general welfare? Is not the im-
petuosity of our passions the continual result, either of habits to which we
addict ourselves from a false calculation, or of ignorance of the means by
which to resist their first impulse, to divert, govern, and direct their action? [20]

Insofar as Condorcet interpreted science in this way, he saw progress, similarly to Descartes, as the overthrow of the past, and looked
upon those who possessed the new dispensation as radically separated
from those who did not. Science was progressive because the discovery
of the only true method of inquiry had opened the way to truths which
would effectively destroy traditional errors and superstitions.

Condorcet's metaphysical interpretation of progress thus contained
the characteristic paradox we have seen so often: against the background of the continuity of past and present, and the inexorable
growth of human understanding, there had taken place the revolutionary adoption of the analytic method and the proclamation of the
rights of man. On the one hand, whatever novelty appeared was
accidental—the uncontrollable presentation to the mind of new sensations. On the other hand, one fixed body of knowledge had wholly
displaced another. Was it the result of new sensations? And if not,
why the break with the past? Auguste Comte pointed to the paradoxical element in Condorcet:

19. *Ibid.*, p. 86.   20. *Ibid.*, p. 352.

The work of Condorcet presents a general and continuous contradiction. On one side it proudly proclaims that civilization in the eighteenth century is infinitely superior to what it was originally. But this sum-total of progress could only be the sum of the partial advances made by civilization in all preceding ages. But, on the other side, in examining successively these different ages, Condorcet presents them almost always as having been, in the last analysis, eras of retrogression. He has on his hands, consequently, a perpetual miracle, and the advance of civilization becomes an effect without a cause.[21]

THE PROGRESS OF METHOD

Condorcet's faith in the future did not rest entirely, however, on the metaphysical argument that progress was necessary. Another strain ran through his theory of progress, the appeal to the history and practice of experimental method, which provided another foundation for the belief in progress. Condorcet, without any doubt, overestimated the extent to which the habit of criticism attributable to science had spread and the ease with which it would spread. And he seems now to have neglected some of the problems that come with the spreading of enlightenment: he assumed that an extension of enlightenment would enrich its quality, rather than tend to cheapen and vulgarize it. But it remains nonetheless true that he provided something of an answer to the questions raised by his sociological account of error by pointing to the sociological fact of progress, the historical development of a coöperative, cumulative, and critical method of inquiry.

It may, of course, be argued that Condorcet took the contemporary state of scientific enlightenment to be simply an empirical illustration of an *a priori* law of progress. There is much in Condorcet that justifies such an interpretation. He wavered constantly between the two interpretations of science, and he did not himself distinguish them from one another. Nevertheless, when, in the *Tenth Epoch,* he endeavored to prove that "nature has fixed no limits to our hopes," he did so explicitly and exclusively on the basis of the nature of the method of science. Even if he took the experimental method of science

21. Quoted by Gillet, *L'Utopie de Condorcet,* p. 135.

to be merely an additional illustration of a fundamental law, it is also true that the illustration stood on its own feet as an argument for progress, and indeed implied a view of progress that was inconsistent with that implied by his metaphysics. The introduction of a new method was of revolutionary significance for progress because it was, uniquely, a method which improved with practice. It made progress a controllable affair, rather than either a necessary or a chance affair; and it made science progressive in the sense that it grew more comprehensive and reliable, and not in the sense that it was established on absolute foundations and moved towards a final Truth. The passage in which this argument appeared is worth quoting at length:

It is then by examining the progression and the laws of this perfection, that we can alone arrive at the knowledge of the extent or boundary of our hopes.

It has never yet been supposed, that all the facts of nature, and all the means of acquiring precision in the computation and analysis of those facts, and all the connections of objects with each other, and all the possible combinations of ideas, can be exhausted by the human mind. The mere relations of magnitude, the combinations, quantity and extent of this idea alone, form already a system too immense for the mind of man ever to grasp the whole of it; a portion, more vast than that which he may have penetrated, will always remain unknown to him. It has, however, been imagined, that, as man can know a part only of the objects which the nature of his intelligence permits him to investigate, he must at length reach the point at which, the number and complication of those he already knows having absorbed all his powers, farther progress will become absolutely impossible.

But, in proportion as facts are multiplied, man learns to class them, and reduce them to more general facts, at the same time that the instruments and methods for observing them, and registering them with exactness, acquire a new precision: in proportion as relations more multifarious between a greater number of objects are discovered, man continues to reduce them to relations of a wider denomination, to express them with greater simplicity, and to present them in a way which may enable a given strength of mind, with a given quantity of attention, to take in a greater number than before: in proportion as the understanding embraces more complicated combinations, a simple mode of announcing these combinations renders them more easy to be treated. Hence it follows that truths, the discovery of which was accompanied with the most laborious efforts, and which at first could not be comprehended but by men of the severest attention, will after a time be unfolded and proved in methods that are not above the efforts of an ordinary capacity. And thus should the methods that led to new combinations be exhausted, should their applications to questions, still unresolved, demand exertions greater than the time or the powers of the learned can bestow, more general methods, means more simple, would soon come to their aid, and open a farther career to genius. The energy, the real extent of human intellect, may remain the same; but the instruments which it can employ will be multiplied and improved; the language which fixes and determines the ideas will acquire more precision and compass; and it will not be here, as in the science of mechanics, where, to increase the force, we must diminish the velocity; on the contrary, the methods by which genius will arrive at the discovery of new truths, augment at once both the force and the rapidity of its operations.

In a word, these changes being themselves the necessary consequences of additional progress in the knowledge of truths of detail, and the cause which produces a demand for new resources, producing at the same time the means of supplying them, it follows that the actual mass of truths appertaining to the sciences of observation, calculation and experiment, may be perpetually augmented, and that without supposing the faculties of man to possess a force and activity, and a scope of action greater than before.[22]

The second argument for progress in Condorcet was thus a return to the type of theory presented by Pascal. Science was progressive not in terms of a metaphysical interpretation, but because its method—the continuing element that holds science together—was a progressing method, resting upon continuity with what had been done as well as upon a critical revision, simplification, and enlargement of received materials.

It was with respect to this method rather than to certain abstract norms, that progress might be measured. The function and significance of historic changes might be determined and evaluated by the measure of their release of the method of science into new fields, and its rise to new capacities. From this point of view, the history of human progress was the story of the conditions that have stimulated and sustained the development of intellectual method, and the systematization and institutionalization of that method in the seventeenth century, so that it gave promise of becoming its own guarantor of further progress. What marked off the "century of philosophy" from other ages was not simply that its enlightenment was more extensive, but that this enlightenment was self-controlling and self-directing. The im-

22. Condorcet, *The Progress of the Human Mind*, pp. 338–41.

measurable superiority of the modern era lay in its having brought to
self-consciousness the fact and the nature of a progressing method of
inquiry.

SCIENCE AND SOCIETY

Condorcet's significant addition to Pascal's more systematic analysis
of progress in science was to call attention to the cultural setting and
incidence of scientific progress. Indeed, where Pascal thought scientific
inquiry properly stopped before it entered certain domains, Condorcet
was convinced that once the institution was well-established, it could
not very easily be insulated from the rest of a culture. Condorcet was
interested in a further question beyond the proof that science was
"progressive" in the sense that it grew broader and more reliable, and
that its method improved with practice. What had this to do with
human progress? What was the relationship of science to happiness
or to society? What was the relationship of progress in knowledge to
moral progress?

Condorcet, no more than others among his contemporaries, regarded
knowledge as an end in itself. Its justification lay in its value for other
purposes. Indeed, he was very well aware that while past history
showed the progress of method, it did not indicate, except in exceptional cases, that scientific progress had been accompanied by the
moral and social improvement of mankind.

We perceive that the exertions of these last ages have done much for the
progress of the human mind, but little for the perfection of the human
species; much for the glory of man, somewhat for his liberty, but scarcely
anything yet for his happiness. . . . The friend of humanity cannot re-
ceive unmixed pleasure but by abandoning himself to the endearing hope
of the future.[23]

The task Condorcet set himself was not simply to show the progress
of knowledge, but also "by what ties nature has indissolubly united
the advancement of knowledge with the progress of liberty, virtue,
and respect for the natural rights of man." [24]

The very way in which Condorcet put the question suggests one of

23. *Ibid.*, pp. 309–10.   24. *Ibid.*, p. 14.

his answers. Science included moral science, which was a set of infallible and universal truths. The principle of equality, for example, might be derived from a first principle, and the art of politics consisted in applying such principles.

After ages of error, after wandering in all the mazes of vague and defective theories, writers upon politics and the law of nations at length arrived at the knowledge of the true rights of man, which they deduced from this simple principle: that *he is a being endowed with sensation, capable of reasoning upon and understanding his interests, and of acquiring moral ideas.*[25]

This interpretation of the nature of moral science raised the question that was central in rationalist-empiricist ethical theory during the century. We have already noted that Condorcet's "sociology of error" raises the question of the connection between the discovery of the "true" moral science and actual moral behavior. The general philosophic issue involved is the question of the relation of reason to value; and Condorcet's position suffers from the weaknesses which Hume pointed out in his critique of the rationalist morality of the eighteenth century. Condorcet's belief in progress, insofar as it was a metaphysical belief, was implicitly based on the assumption, for instance, that human beings will prefer truth to error, once they have discovered it, an assumption which brings in the non-rational factors of preference, inclination, or will.

But this was not Condorcet's entire answer to the question of the relationship of science to social progress. It is significant that the very passage in which Condorcet argued that all errors in politics and morals go back to errors in physics was followed immediately by another argument in which equality was justified because it was modelled upon the practicing morality of science. "This progress of the physical sciences, . . . wherein it is not thought that birth, profession, or appointment have given a right to judge what the individual is not in a situation to understand . . . exhibits at every step the model they [politics and morals] ought to follow." [26] This emphasis on the method of science rather than on the presumed absolute moral rules which it discovers considerably alters the problem of the connection of reason and value. Moral values like equality become justifiable not

25. *Ibid.*, p. 231.   26. *Ibid.*, pp. 298–300.

as inferences from a natural law but because their worth is demonstrated by the success of an actual institution, scientific method, in which they are incorporated. In short, Condorcet pointed to the fact that scientific progress offered an actual model, exciting men to revise their social moralities, and providing a standard in the light of which progress might be measured. If physical science had not promoted human happiness it was because social morality had not yet taken the cue. In the fact that the scientific community had a morality—a method —in which progress was inherent lay the importance of scientific progress for controlled social change.

Condorcet argued on behalf of the unlimited extension of enlightenment because publicity and equality were tested values integral to scientific practice and progress. Men ought to be educated because the method of science at once sustained and thrived upon the interplay of many minds.[27] In the century and a half since Condorcet wrote we have had of course to confront the fact that democratic publicity has led in many areas to a confusion of the popular, the cheap, and the attainable, with the reasonable. As Professor Morris Cohen, for example, observed, "Reason lost ground because of the spread of literacy. . . . The spread of literacy, without the prolonged discipline on which aristocracies must depend for the maintenance of their powers and privileges, diluted the intellectual life and brought about a flabby popularity not conducive to rigorous reason." [28]

But what Condorcet had to say about the principle of equality as an extension of scientific practice to other human relationships was nevertheless not unsuggestive. For, as Professor Cohen goes on to remark, the extension of democracy has also brought gains to the intellectual realm, "e.g., increased respect for hitherto undignified facts." The awareness of a problem and the ability to locate it are necessary conditions of its solution; and while the dogma that certain things are beneath mention, and that certain classes may rightly be excluded from sharing in a culture, may help keep reason pure, it will also keep reason insulated. If we take the worst view, Demos may be unable to do more than contribute a yelp of pain when he feels the pinch; but that something is pinching may be very valuable information. Pub-

27. See, for example, *ibid.*, pp. 342–43.
28. Cohen, *Reason and Nature*, p. 6.

licity and equality are at least conditions, as Condorcet suggested, for enlarging the area in which intelligent inquiry may be carried on; and, as such, they may react back upon inquiry and enrich it even in those areas where it is already well-established.

Condorcet's conviction that, in the future, truth, virtue, and happiness would be indissolubly connected thus stemmed in part from the fact that his notion of virtue was controlled by the values operative in the pursuit of truth. The virtue of science was exhibited by its power in the physical sciences; and if employed in morality and politics, it could enjoy similar success. The connection of progress in knowledge with social progress lay in the power of scientific method to uphold new values, subversive of the old, and integral to the progress of intelligence. In science we have the example of a continuous and critical process of learning. The organization of science was thus a model of a progressive community, and the introduction of the method of science into politics, morals, and religion therefore gave promise of human perfectibility.

THE SOCIALIZATION OF SCIENCE

Condorcet's unshakable optimism concerning the future grew out of his metaphysical assurance concerning the *necessity* of progress. Although, as we have seen, his belief in progress depended in some measure on his analysis of the nature of scientific method, this would not in itself have been sufficient to support a belief that progress was absolutely assured. Other conditions were obviously required. If science brought progress, either certain social conditions or certain metaphysical laws were necessary to support the expectation that science could, or would, be practised freely. On the whole, Condorcet turned to metaphysics to buttress his belief in progress, enunciating a doctrine purporting to prove that the laws of nature were peculiarly propitious for the practice of science. The real world was nothing but the world of the physicist, which consequently guaranteed the relevance and progress of science.

This reductive dogma and others like it have since been called "scientism." But "scientism" is a metaphysical doctrine extrinsic to experimental methods, and while it has undoubtedly had a powerful influence, it should not be regarded as the only effect of these experimental methods upon habits of thought. Indeed, Condorcet's own arguments were not exclusively "scientistic," and if we so regard them, we overlook some of the values of his argument, some of the facts to which he pointed, and important implications of these facts. For Condorcet's optimism also rested on an historical appraisal of the strength the scientific method had gained in his culture.

The progress of science depended, for Condorcet, upon certain factors in the environment of science. Negatively, scientific progress in any field depended upon freedom from the *esprit de système* and external authority. Positively, scientific progress depended on experimental methods, and upon the growing acceptance in and through practice of the value of free criticism. Condorcet thought that the new scientific method was antipathetic to the *esprit de système,* and would, as it extended itself to new problems, gradually subvert it. As for external authority, Condorcet believed the method of science to be too well domesticated and the respect for its authority to have already spread too widely in his own time to permit its prolonged suppression by outside forces.

It was through his interpretation of science in terms of its method, and through his insight that this method was a socialized habit of mind, shared by a community of investigators and critics who exhibited a distinctive morality of their own, that Condorcet suggested a way of eliminating the apparently radical disjuncture of irrational "custom" and the appeal of ideal "nature." For if science was not so much a passive and static body of finished truths as an active temper of mind, if it was primarily an organized way of asking questions and of making and holding judgments, then it might itself be regarded as a custom, and might, if the effort were made, become itself a kind of "second nature."

In thus regarding science as a form of social activity, Condorcet also reformulated the problem of its relationship to other kinds of social behavior. Science was model social behavior, in which the pernicious doctrine that men were separated into classes to which different moralities were proper was eliminated. Consequently, there was a way of seeing beyond the necessity, which seemed to be involved by one aspect of Condorcet's "sociology of error," that the new enlightenment must itself in its turn be perverted to the special interests of an oppressing class. Condorcet's "sociology of error" had argued that a social class tends after a while to employ the instruments it possesses simply to maintain itself. But the emergence of science had made possible the emergence of a new kind of social class, with a distinctive kind of class-interest. For while, like other classes, it might be interested simply in maintaining and promoting the necessary conditions for its continued existence, the conditions for maintaining a class of informed and responsible critics were significantly different. Equality, publicity, and freedom from external domination were dynamic affairs, and a class whose interest was defined by them would be under the practical necessity of enlarging itself and extending these conditions to others. For such a class, "enlightened self-interest" would be the interest of enlightened selves in further enlightenment.

It is, of course, fairly easy to show that Condorcet's expectations concerning the probability of progress have not been justified. There is no doubt that he overestimated the strength of the new habits created by scientific criticism, and underestimated the social and psychological obstacles in the way of extending the morality implicit in scientific practice to everyday human problems. Indeed, to a large extent Condorcet's own interpretation of science, as well as many later interpretations, was an illustration of the strength of older, unconscious habits of mind.

Yet if it is easy to show that Condorcet was an enthusiast, it is equally easy to make too much of his "optimism" and "naïveté." For while he may have been overly optimistic concerning the speed with which scientific methods would be employed to help in the development of new social moralities, he did not actually go very far astray in his estimate of the disruptive effect of the new habit of organized criticism upon older moralities. The very attempts which, since Condorcet's time, have been made to limit or stifle free inquiry into social conditions illustrate not only the power of inherited habits, but the rise of a new kind of social authority in which "change" and "progress" are integral and appealing elements. It is significant that many modern techniques of repression have had to employ the label "scientific," and that they have had to pretend to be "new," "progressive," and "in tune with the times." Whatever may have been his appraisal of its consequences, Condorcet was aware of a fundamental change in social processes due to the emergence in European society of an inherently expansive institution which had control over its own growth.

It is for this reason that Condorcet may still have something to say to us. For the problems generated by the impact of scientific institutions on our modes of life cannot be satisfied by passing easy judgments on Condorcet's predictions, or by making predictions ourselves concerning the probable drift of events. These problems are initially problems of controlling events through choice, and they require an estimate of the possibilities inherent in existing institutions. In this regard, Condorcet's vision may be worth recapturing. In our time as well as his, it is a significant element in the situation of those of us who wish to direct our activities by conscious choices that we possess an institutionalized method of action which, in its own terms, is progressive. This provides no proof that social progress is guaranteed, nor even an assurance that it is probable, but it suggests a possibility —that social progress is measurable by the extent to which the conditions of free inquiry become pervasive and entrenched, and that it may take place if and where those conditions are employed to direct social behavior.

A Summing Up

UNLIKE those in an industrial age whose belief in progress rested on the physical powers of science, the *philosophes* were primarily interested in the immediate moral implications of the scientific enterprise.]Their vision of science was essentially that for which Descartes supplied the major impulse: they were interested in science as Method, as a systematic procedure for distinguishing the true from the false. Science was Enlightenment, the questioning and illumination of all beliefs by the individual's "natural light." For the *philosophes* as for Descartes, Method was not simply a limited technique to be used only on specified occasions, but a universal instrument of criticism and a new morality of action, something to be assimilated into the daily habits of the individual and society. As Descartes had said, each and every advance in science was to be esteemed not so much for its own sake as for its contribution to the perfecting of Method.

Within this broad view, however, different conceptions of the nature of science and enlightenment were possible. As we have seen, two divergent theories of progress were really present in the works of the *philosophes,* and a brief summary may help us to bring their differences into focus and to consider the issues between them.

The primary source of the first theory of progress lies in Descartes. While Descartes had made it plain that the choice of his Method was the choice of a way of behaving, he had also made it plain that the justification of this Method lay not only in its fruits, though these were great, but in the unprovisional truth of the principles on which it was based. Unless he were to involve himself in a logical circle, Descartes could not use his mathematical method to discover or establish these principles: rather, these principles provided an antecedent guarantee that his mathematical method was the exclusive agency of intellectual

and moral progress. Descartes fixed the conviction upon later generations that the methods of science require an external guarantee. His
Method was more than simply the orderly analysis of problems into
their simple elements, or the systematic application of mathematics to
all spheres: it was these techniques plus the metaphysical propositions
that made their conclusions absolute and exclusive.

It was in this way that the conception of science and enlightenment
came to connote not only an habitual attitude of critical inquiry but a
set of absolute beliefs upon which inquiry and action must rest, and
which are not themselves modifiable by further inquiry. While the
philosophes employed the empiricist language of Locke, their empiricism remained essentially Cartesian and rationalistic, retaining the
conviction that the particular grammar in terms of which they chose
to express their experience was the only grammar nature used. The
philosophes tended to think of reason and enlightenment as a system
of simple, indubitable, and eternal truths, and through their metaphysical "experimental physics of the soul" they attempted to provide
an external framework for the interpretation of human inquiry and
progress.

The consequence was a theory of progress which, paradoxically,
recapitulated in a different language the main features of the theological interpretation of history which the *philosophes* were combating.
The emergence of science became either the product of a revelation, a
sudden discovery without historical antecedents, and carrying its own
certificate of validity, or it became the culmination of a process in
which all evil was not really or finally evil, and all errors were necessary steps in the improvement of mankind. The harmonious order of
nature emerged as a thinner version of Providence.

This interpretation of the conclusions of science apart from its selective methods, and in terms of the metaphysical belief in a necessary
order of reason, was responsible for the dualistic elements in the
theories of progress developed by the *philosophes*. For what did not
meet the standards of reason, what, for example, did not follow the
natural, reasonable order of the development of ideas out of sensations,
had to be assigned to the sphere of accident and dis-order. Thus,
D'Alembert, following suggestions in Condillac, distinguished between the "metaphysical" account of progress, which exhibited the

"necessary," and therefore intelligible, itinerary of "the isolated spirit," and the "historical" account of the succession of ideas, which simply recapitulated the accidental order in which ideas had happened to succeed one another. This was an order which was distorted by the accident of social organization and the influence of the past. The actual history of progress was thus separated from the eternal principles that made progress natural and necessary.

This separation of philosophy and reason from history and experience was, of course, an extraordinarily effective weapon when it was used, for example by Voltaire, to show that history was an almost unbroken lapse from reason, and that there was, despite high-sounding rationalizations and claims to universality, an inevitable element of irrational preference or local prejudice in any human judgment. The idea of reason gave the histories written during the Enlightenment a further philosophic and critical import. The philosopher-historians of the Enlightenment, whose appeal to reason expressed a concern to extricate the underlying unity from the variety of details, were convinced that a mere narrative of the order in which individual events had followed one another explained nothing, and, indeed, did not quite do what it pretended to be doing. The *philosophes* were acutely conscious of the role of selection in the writing of histories, both in those of their opponents and in their own, and they felt that no history could in fact be merely a chronicle, but had to involve some general principles of selection. If it was to explain anything, history had to be a phase of science and philosophy: it had to employ general laws, and be illuminated by insight into constant factors in human conduct and perennial moral truths.

It was, however, the very interpretation of reason as a set of metaphysical and eternal truths which prevented the integration of philosophy and history, and introduced the paradoxes into the *philosophes'* theories of progress. Reason was formulated in terms which were explicitly disengaged from the historical process itself. A metaphysical psychology and theory of natural rights described what would have happened had not history, change, and the contingent intervened. Given this theory, the issue for the *philosophes* was not to explain how progress had come about, but, indeed, why it had not come about.

The idea of reason as a set of unassailable metaphysical truths produced a paradoxical theory of progress because it interpreted scientific
criticism and inquiry as instruments in the realization of ideals or
goals that were not themselves subject to further inquiry or parts of a
progressive process. The consequence was that ends and means were
separated, ends being assigned to a realm of necessity, while means
were left in the realm of the contingent. The relation between ends
and means thus became purely mechanical. The connection between
any particular means and a given end was interpreted as only adventi-
tious and temporary: in another situation, another means might ac-
complish the same end. The mechanistic interpretation of the relation
of means and ends, which holds that a means may produce a given
end without itself being among the actual ingredients present in the
outcome, is thus the expression of a kind of surreptitious supernaturalism in which the end is in the last analysis guaranteed, while
the particular means employed can be blamed on the accidents of
history. So even the crimes and follies of the past might lead to the
reign of reason, nature, and humanity.

There was present in the theories of the *philosophes,* however, the
suggestion of a view that offered an alternative to these paradoxes. In
Rousseau's protests against the narrowness of the empiricist views of
human experience, in Diderot's attacks upon mechanistic interpretations of matter and thought, and in his biological and evolutionary
insights, paths were broken that moved beyond the emphasis of rationalist empiricism on the necessity for predetermined goals and an
antecedent metaphysical guarantee. And there ran through the reflections of many of the *philosophes* the recognition, exemplified by
Pascal, that the method of science was unique among intellectual
authorities in that it was a cumulative and self-corrective process.
When the conditions and impact of this method were explored and
dramatized by the philosopher-historians, the conception of social
progress as the extension of the habit of free inquiry was developed.

To many there is, of course, something unsatisfactory in this dismissal of the necessity for a higher metaphysical or moral justification
of science. If the conclusions reached by scientific method are to be
checked only by other conclusions reached by the same method, are
we not involved in a logical circle? How do we know that the method

itself is reliable? It is only from the point of view of the Cartesian demand for certainty and finality, however, that such questions must be
answered by demonstrating that science rests on absolutely firm
foundations. The Cartesian proof that science was a progressive agency
had been that scientific knowledge was progressive because its absolute reliability had been established on higher grounds. In contrast,
what was implied in this second view of science was that scientific
knowledge was reliable because it was indefinitely progressive. Scientific knowledge was progressive not because it rested on unprovisionally true premises, but precisely because the truths it established were
all provisional, the means to new investigations, and subject to test
and enlargement by further inquiry.

To the contemporary "problem" of the so-called "irresponsibility"
of science a similar answer may be made. Free inquiry becomes servile
and irresponsible only when it is subordinated to external goals which
are not themselves held to be within its domain. Inquiry does not "invent" values; it must find them where they are, in custom, tradition,
the arts, and creative experience. But it is only the introduction of the
progressive methods of organized inquiry that makes the moralities
that grow out of these values progressive. In short, from the point of
view of this interpretation of the relation of science to progress, scientific method does not need the justification of a higher morality: it is
our moralities which require the kind of integrated growth which is
exemplified where the method of science is employed.

The general disrepute into which the dogma of necessary progress
has fallen has cast a cloud not only over those elements in the beliefs
of the *philosophes* which may be defensible, but over the liberal philosophy in which the belief in human betterment through the use of intelligence is a central part. The scientist and the humanist are today
held to be at odds, the one irresponsible, the other impotent. There are
those who hold that the belief in the powers of intelligence shows a
failure in imagination, or a loss of a "tragic sense of life," and the man
who holds that scientific method provides the most reliable way of
obtaining truths and controlling conduct may find himself accused of
"scientism," or even of "rationalism."

Under these circumstances, it is worth remembering that the *philosophes* thought that reason and humanity were one. Undoubtedly,

their rationalism was sometimes dogmatic and shallow, though not so often as is sometimes alleged. But where they failed it was essentially a failure of imagination, and this failure of imagination was not due to their attachment to science, but to a metaphysical theory which exalted the categories of physics into the exclusive properties of nature, and told them beforehand the kind of thing they could expect to find, and the properties of things they would have to reject as secondary and illusory. The separation of science and humanism is a consequence of this metaphysics. But the *philosophes* also succeeded in transcending this rigid idea of reason. They brought science and humanism together by showing that the values incorporated into the methods of reason were also the values that were basic if the pursuit of any other values was to be stabilized and controlled. It was the *philosophes* who laid the foundations for the conviction that the moral significance of science lies in the opportunity its methods present to develop responsible and informed uses of social power, and they are largely responsible for the liberal faith that freedom of thought, equality, and coöperative inquiry are ingredients of any progressive morality.

Selected Bibliography

I

Alembert, Jean le Rond d'. Discours préliminaire de l'*Encyclopédie*. Ed. by F. Picavet. Paris:1894.
—— Œuvres philosophiques, historiques et littéraires. Ed. by J. F. Bastien. Paris:1805.
Chastellux, F. J. de. De la félicité publique. Paris:1822.
Condillac, Etienne Bonnot de. Œuvres. Paris:1798.
Condorcet, M. J. A. N. de. Esquisse d'un tableau historique des progrès de l'esprit humain. Ed. by O. H. Prior. Paris:1933.
—— Œuvres. Paris:1847–49.
—— Outlines of an Historical View of the Progress of the Human Mind. Tr. from the French. London:1795.
Descartes, René. Discours de la méthode. Ed. by E. Gilson. Paris:1925.
—— Œuvres. Ed. by C. Adam and P. Tannery. Paris:1897–1913.
—— Philosophical Works. Tr. by E. S. Haldane and G. R. T. Ross. Cambridge:1931.
Diderot, Denis. Diderot, Interpreter of Nature: selected writings. Ed. by J. Kemp, tr. by J. Stewart and J. Kemp. New York:1938.
—— Œuvres complètes. Ed. by J. Assézat and M. Tourneux. Paris:1875–79.
Duclos, C. P. "Considérations sur les mœurs de ce siècle," "Mémoires sur le règne de Louis XV," Œuvres complètes, Vols. I, III. Paris:1821.
Fontenelle, B. le Bovier de. Œuvres. Paris:1825.
Helvétius, Claude Adrien. De l'esprit. Paris:1880.
—— A Treatise on Man. Tr. by W. Hooper. London:1777.
Holbach, Paul Henri d'. Ethocratie. Amsterdam:1776.
—— La Politique naturelle. London:1773.
—— Nature and Her Laws (Système de la nature). Tr. from the French. London:1816.
Locke, John. Essay concerning Human Understanding. Ed. by A. C. Fraser. Oxford:1894.
Malebranche, N. De la recherche de la vérité. Ed. by F. Bouillier. Paris:1880.

Pascal, Blaise. De l'autorité en matière de philosophie. Ed. by L. Robert. Paris:1886.

──── Œuvres. Ed. by L. Brunschvicg and E. Boutroux. Paris:1904–14.

──── Pensées. Tr. by W. F. Trotter. New York:1941.

Rousseau, Jean-Jacques. Emile. Tr. by B. Foxley. London:1910.

──── The Social Contract and Discourses. Tr. by G. D. H. Cole. London: 1913.

Turgot, A. R. J. Œuvres. Paris:1808–11.

──── On the Progress of the Human Mind. Tr. by McQ. de Grange. Hanover:1929.

──── The Life and Writings of Turgot. Ed. by W. W. Stephens. London, New York:1895.

Volney, C. F. C. de. The Law of Nature, or Catechism of French Citizens. Tr. from the French. London:1796.

──── The Ruins. Tr. from the French. London:1811.

Voltaire, F. M. A. de. Works. Tr. by T. Smollett, T. Francklin, and others. London:1761.

II

Babbitt, Irving. Rousseau and Romanticism. Boston:1919.

Barni, J. R. Les Moralistes français au dix-huitième siècle. Paris:1904.

Bayet, A. and Albert, F., eds. Les Ecrivains politiques du dix-huitième siècle: extraits. Paris:1904.

Becker, Carl. The Heavenly City of the Eighteenth-Century Philosophers. New Haven:1932.

Belin, J. P. Le Mouvement philosophique de 1748 à 1789. Paris:1913.

Bertrand, J. D'Alembert. Paris:1889.

Billy, André. Diderot. Paris:1932.

Bouillier, F. Histoire de la philosophie cartésienne. Paris:1868.

Boutroux, Emile. Pascal. Tr. by E. M. Creak. Manchester:1902.

Brunet, Pierre. L'Introduction des théories de Newton en France au dix-huitième siècle avant 1738. Paris:1931.

Brunetière, F. Etudes critiques sur l'histoire de la littérature française, 1ᵉ, 3ᵉ, 5ᵉ séries. Paris:1888, 1890, 1893.

Brunschvicg, Leon. René Descartes. Paris:1937.

──── Pascal. Paris:1932.

──── Spinoza et ses contemporains. Paris:1923.

Bury, J. B. The Idea of Progress. London:1924.

Cahen, L. Condorcet et la révolution française. Paris:1904.

──── Consistance de Voltaire le philosophe. Paris:1938.

Carré, J. R. La Philosophie de Fontenelle. Paris:1932.

Cassirer, Ernst. "Das Problem Jean-Jacques Rousseau," *Archiv für Geschichte der Philosophie,* XLI (1932).

———— Die Philosophie der Aufklärung. Tübingen:1932.

———— Rousseau, Kant. Goethe. Tr. by J. Gutmann, P. O. Kristeller, and J. H. Randall. Princeton:1945.

Cohen, M. R. Reason and Nature. New York:1931.

Dakin, Douglas. Turgot and the Ancient Regime in France. London:1913.

Damiron, J. P. Mémoires pour servir à l'histoire de la philosophie au dix-huitième siècle. Paris:1858.

Delvaille, J. Histoire de l'idée de progrès jusqu'à la fin du dix-huitième siècle. Paris:1910.

Desnoiresterres, G. Voltaire et la société francaişe au dix-huitième siècle. Paris:1871–76.

Dewey, John. The Quest for Certainty. New York:1929.

Ducros, Louis. Les Encyclopédistes. Paris:1900.

———— French Society in the Eighteenth Century. Tr. by W. de Geiger. London:1926.

Fabre, Joseph. Les pères de la révolution. Paris:1910.

Faguet, Emile. Dix-huitième siècle. Paris:1890.

Flint, Robert. History of the Philosophy of History. New York:1894.

Gibson, A. Boyce. The Philosophy of Descartes. London:1932.

Gillet, Mathurin. L'Utopie de Condorcet. Paris:1883.

Gillot, Hubert. Denis Diderot. Paris:1937.

———— La Querelle des anciens et des modernes en France. Paris:1914.

Gilson, Etienne. Etudes sur le rôle de la pensée médiévale dans la formation du système cartésien. Paris:1930.

Grossman, M. The Philosophy of Helvetius. New York:1926.

Hearnshaw, F. J. C., ed. Political and Social Theories of Some Great French Thinkers of the Enlightenment. London:1930.

Hendel, C. W. Jean-Jacques Rousseau, Moralist. New York:1934.

Höffding, Harald. Jean-Jacques Rousseau and His Philosophy. Tr. by W. Richards and J. C. Saidler. London: 1930.

Hubert, René. Les Sciences sociales dans l'*Encyclopédie*. Paris:1923.

———— Rousseau et l'*Encyclopédie*. Paris:1928.

Jones, R. F. Ancients and Moderns: a study of the background of the battle of the books. St. Louis:1936.

Keeling, S. V. Descartes. London:1934.

Lanson, Gustave. "L'Influence de la philosophie cartésienne sur la littérature française," "Le Rôle de l'expérience dans la formation de la philosophie du dix-huitième siècle," Etudes d'histoire littéraire. Paris:1929.

———— Manuel bibliographique de la littérature française moderne, XVIe, XVIIe, XVIIIe, et XIXe siècles. Paris:1931.

———— "Origines et premières manifestations de l'esprit philosophique dans la littérature française de 1675 à 1748," Revue des Cours et Conférences (1908–9, 1909–10).

———— Voltaire. Paris:1906.

Lenoir, R. Condillac. Paris:1924.

LeRoy, G. La Psychologie de Condillac. Paris:1937.

Lovejoy, A. O. The Great Chain of Being. Cambridge:1942.

Maritain, Jacques. The Dream of Descartes, together with Some Other Essays. Tr. by M. L. Andison. New York:1944.

—— Three Reformers: Luther, Descartes, Rousseau. New York:1929.

Martin, Kingsley. French Liberal Thought in the Eighteenth Century. Boston:1929.

Morley, John. Critical Miscellanies. London:1888.

—— Diderot and the Encyclopedists. London:1914.

—— Rousseau. London:1873.

—— Voltaire. London:1923.

Mornet, Daniel. French Thought in the Eighteenth Century. Tr. by L. M. Levin. New York:1929.

—— Les Origines intellectuelles de la révolution française. Paris:1933.

Picavet, F. Les Idéologues. Paris:1891.

Pellisson, Maurice. Les Hommes de lettres au dix-huitième siècle. Paris: 1911.

Plekhanov, G. V. Essays in the History of Materialism. Tr. by R. Fox. London:1934.

Robinet, A. Condorcet, sa vie, son œuvre. Paris:1911.

Rosenkranz, J. Diderots Leben und Werke. Leipzig:1866.

Roustan, M. The Pioneers of the French Revolution. Tr. by F. Whyte. London:1925.

Sabine, G. H. A History of Political Theory. New York:1937.

Say, Leon. Turgot. Tr. by M. E. Anderson. Chicago:1888.

Schapiro, J. S. Condorcet and the Rise of Liberalism. New York:1934.

Schaupp, Zora. The Naturalism of Condillac. Bryn Mawr:1925.

Schelle, G. Turgot. Paris:1909.

Sée, Henri. Les Idées politiques en France au dix-huitième siècle. Paris: 1920.

Strowski, F. Pascal et son temps. Paris:1907.

Torrey, Norman L. Rousseau's Quarrel with Grimm and Diderot. New Haven:1943.

—— and Gordon, D. H. The Censoring of Diderot's Encyclopédie and the Re-established Text. New York:1947.

—— The Spirit of Voltaire. New York:1938.

—— Voltaire and the Enlightenment. New York:1931.

Whitehead, A. N. Science and the Modern World. New York:1939.

Wickwar, W. H. Baron D'Holbach: a prelude to the French Revolution. London:1935.

Windelband, Wilhelm. A History of Philosophy. Tr. by J. H. Tufts. London:1914.

Wright, E. H. The Meaning of Rousseau. London:1929.

Index

Vita

Charles Frankel, born, New York City, December 13, 1917. Attended New York public schools; graduated, Townsend Harris High School, June, 1932; entered Columbia College, September, 1933, graduated, June, 1937. A.B. with Honors in English and Philosophy. Passed final examination for Ph.D., May, 1942, Ph.D. conferred, 1946. Susan Linn Sage Scholar in Philosophy, Cornell University, 1937–38; University Scholar, Residence Scholar, Columbia University, 1938–39; Lecturer, Instructor in Philosophy, Columbia University, 1939–47 (on leave, 1942–46); Woodbridge Prize in Philosophy, 1946–47; Assistant Professor of Philosophy, 1947. Member, Phi Beta Kappa, American Philosophical Association. General Editor, *Introduction to Contemporary Civilization, A Source Book* (2 vols., New York, 1941); editor, Jean-Jacques Rousseau, *The Social Contract* (New York, 1947); author, "The Enlightenment," "The Expansion of Liberalism, 1870 to the Present," "The Growth of Socialism, 1870 to the Present," and other articles in *Manual for Contemporary Civilization* (2 vols., New York, 1941–42); contributor to *The American Scholar, The Journal of Philosophy,* and other periodicals.